Robert T. Sicora

612-251-7766

robtsicora@gmail.com

Y0-AWH-027

Sync and Swim is the book you SHOULD HAVE READ in your MBA program. The dynamics revealed here are the most important factors in developing a competitive business. All companies must develop a strategy around them to succeed, especially in today's markets.

Jack Tesmer describes the most critical organizing factors for success. Identifying the kind of competitive environment in which a business takes place and the appropriate organizational culture and structure is a major part of business strategy. We overlook these dimensions at our peril as they often are the difference between success and failure in the marketplace.

Sync & Swim acquaints you with the four kinds of competitive markets and the organizational pattern that best supports business done in those markets. Reading this book will not only acquaint you with these market types but also lead you through an examination of your marketplace position and the viability of success that you can expect from engaging in business within it.

I have used the concepts in Sync and Swim in my everyday business life for many years. The very simple idea of "understand the product for your market (external) and then install and practice everything in your organization (internal) to "match" that market" is maybe the most profound and useful thought process to come along this century.

Anthony Rotondi, Formerly CEO and CIO, Assurant Insurance, RTW Insurance Co., The Jack Tesmer Institute, APU INC., Thomas Anthony Group, The Rotondi Group

Jack Tesmer's model helps to provide clarity on the development of the right business strategy and organizational structure/culture needed to successfully have a profitable enterprise. The 2 X 2 model helps leaders to get to simplicity from the far side of complexity and to be better able to position their organizations for success. Clearly an organization must have the right strategy, organization and culture to align ("Sync") with the markets targeted by the business to be successful.

I just used your book 2 weeks ago, as a reference with our CIO on the importance of process improvement and systems integration along with the need for cost management to effectively operate in our jungle environment. I also used it as part of a strategic vision presentation I made to our Executive Committee.

Daniel Haag, Sundt Construction, SVP and Chief Administrative Officer. Employee-owned Sundt Construction is one of the oldest and largest general contractors in the nation.

I worked with Jack for several years in Merck Sharp & Dohme in several European countries and Jack's ideas, expertise and facilitational leadership were instrumental in introducing the organizational changes necessary for our company to successfully compete in the diverse markets in which we operated. The concepts and strategies developed by Jack over many years are relevant and applicable to success in today's marketplace and I would recommend the book to any executive trying to analyze and make sense of the markets in which they operate.

Sync or Swim is a user friendly model whereby business leaders create their own business strategy and decisions for their future. The model allows leaders to determine the position of their business within the market place they serve, the ramifications of that position, and the position that they desire to achieve. Leaders come to an understanding of those things that they can change and those which they do not control and to which they must adapt. In the end, business leaders are able to create a strategic plan to maximize their position in the marketplace. The process is applicable to small, medium and large sized companies. Larger companies with multiple markets must create business plans for each of their individual markets to integrate into their overall strategic plan. I have been personally involved in aiding companies to use this model to assess their situations and to create successful strategic plans for their future

Paul Pelkola, Organization Development Manager, 3M Retired

To think outside the box, innovators need to create their own new boxes. Jack Tesmer has certainly done that in his latest book: <u>Sync & Swim</u>. First he reviews his well validated conclusion that in order for firms to "swim" well in today's rapidly changing and complex environments, they must "synchronize" all the precisely assessed dimensions of their organizations with those of their chosen markets. Tesmer's market-centric box-approach to strategic management is painted with memorable metaphors. But what distinguishes this new book is Tesmer's focus on providing candid advice and concrete examples of exactly how to manage organizational change. Highlighted are the needs for different kinds of leadership styles and structures. These chapters can obviously be of immense and immediate value to MBA students, managers, executives, and change coaches/consultants competing in the business sector. However, throughout the last half of <u>Sync & Swim</u> I kept thinking how well Tesmer's advice could be applied also to non-profit organizations, so many of which find themselves today "sinking" by not "syncing."

David L. Christopherson, PhD – *Hamline University School of Business – St. Paul, Minnesota*

Jack Tesmer comes throiiugh in a wonderful way inhis latest book. I have personally tested his skills with two Fortune 500 firms and what he has to say works! Buy the book and explore the real meaning of an organization.

Jim Lane, retired, V.P. Snap-on OEM Group, Corporate Snap-on, Kenosha, WI.

In the real world where the use of real management tools is needed to produce real results, Jack Tesmer's analysis and portrayal of the market archetypes and the need to continually adjust or reconfigure our organizations to match their corresponding market environment is very insightful. In particular, I found his business evaluation methods qnd specific strategies to steer, survive, and succeed with the various market environments to be useful—not just interesting, but useful in a pragmatic, day to day business operation. Understanding the dynamic interrelationships between organizations and markets, and employing the necessary tools to keep them in synchronization is a key element to maintaining viability and profitability.

Ken Owens, CEO, DHY Corporation, Lakeville, MN

SYNC & SWIM!

SYNC & SWIM!

How to gain Mastery over the dynamics of competition

JACK TESMER

TESMER
CREATIVE ARTS

Library of Congress Control Number: 2014919695
ISBN: Hardcover   978-1-5035-1272-6
                 Softcover   978-1-5035-1273-3
                 eBook   978-1-5035-1274-0

Rev. date: 01/16/2015

To order additional copies of this book, contact:
Xlibris
1-888-795-4274
www.Xlibris.com
Orders@Xlibris.com
540604

CONTENTS

PART ONE

The Fascinating Dynamics of the Competitive Market

PART TWO

Arranging the Organization to Compete

PART THREE

A Guide to the Four Markets

PART FOUR

Transforming Your Organization

PART FIVE

Leading the Twenty-First Century Organization

NOTE TO THE READER

The purpose of my original book *Your Perfect Business Match* was to expose managers and those who teach and consult with them to a new and powerful yet simple model of the competitive dynamics that govern business formation, strategy, and organization development.

This model, with its many interesting and useful dynamics, was developed from my experience over some thirty years of consulting all over the world, both as an independent practitioner and as the head of organization development at 3M for ten years.

I now have the opportunity, provided by Xlibris, to reissue the book with some additions and changes that will be useful to entrepreneurs, managers, consultants, and MBA professors and students in their pursuit of excellence in strategy formulation and organizational development.

I have learned a considerable amount by writing and publishing *Your Perfect Business Match*. I have incorporated that learning in this book and have provided some examples of actual companies as they pursued their strategic journey.

Several of my colleagues have indicated that the process of examining the market position and the organizational match is a breakthrough in strategic thinking. Examining the competitive market position and matching that with an organizational response do not displace what many others have developed over the last fifty years; rather, it provides a context for incorporating many of the models developed by strategic thinkers.

The purpose of this edition is to provide the reader with some clear and understandable ways of getting agreements in their companies with which to build strategy and an organization that has potential for supporting the business over the long run.

Any manager, at any level, will benefit by using these clear and simple views of the business and the organization as a common ground with their businesses. Reaching agreement on these fundamentals is crucial to our present-day business environments.

ACKNOWLEDGEMENTS

I have spent nearly twenty-five years in developing these ideas, with the help of others, chief among whom are the following:

Frans van Lier, dear friend and freelance reporter in Amsterdam, whose article concerning the seminal ideas of the book was published in the *Holland Financial Times* of Amsterdam and whose further initiatives began publishing the process in Europe in the early 1990s.

Tony Rotondi, also a dear friend and master networker, former CEO and CIO in a large insurance company, who first insisted that the book needed to be written and who has partnered with me continuously since.

David Christopherson, PhD, has consistently encouraged me from an academic point of view and has used and developed the material for undergraduates and graduate students.

Manuel Fernandes of Lisbon, Portugal, who has been a close colleague and fellow developer and has also collaborated on interesting and useful additional processes for managers and entrepreneurs.

Frank Hoy, director, Collaborative for Entrepreneurship and Innovation, School of Business; Paul R. Beswick Professor of Innovation and Entrepreneurship, Worcester Polytechnic Institute.

Steve Werner, Tom Eckstein, Ben Nieters, John LeTourneau, Kathleen Pytlieski, and others who have provided assistance in many ways.

I am also thankful to the students at the Carlson School of the University of Minnesota, Hamline University, and St. Cloud State University, along with students in several European countries, for their participation.

There are several thousand managers, mainly in small to medium-sized companies, who have experienced the process in the last twenty years, including one thousand managers from Portugal who participated in a study of organizational types in that country in 2002. From that study, we were able to predict some of the conditions that presently are part of the business experience in that country and others like it.

FOREWORD

One of the big lessons that came out of the wars of the last fifty years is that warfare had become asymmetrical—that is, unpredictable in design and scope and therefore should not be engaged in with the same strategies and tactics used in WWI and II, Korea, and possibly Vietnam. Now anyone can be an enemy and can do significant damage, alone or together, anywhere, in crowded cities and open fields, in battlefields, and behind the lines. There no longer is a place for battle; it happens anywhere.

The reason that was so important to the army is that in order to engage and be successful, the new army needed to be able to operate optimally at all times and in any place. Warfare needed a very different army with different strategies and tactics. And thus the armed services went through immense changes. There really was no option but to change.

This is an excellent example of what many call contingency theory, which suggests that *all organizational design needs to fit the kind of environment in which the primary activity takes place.* There is no "one size fits all," which was prevalent in the days of Henry Ford and the auto industry for so long. The top performance of any system is possible only when there is an appropriate design—that is, a design that *fits* the kind of competitive work or activity that takes place.

The marketplace has changed just as much as the battlefield! The market has also become asymmetrical, where business is done anywhere, anytime, unpredictably, globally. New products are suddenly available often without warning; companies enter markets with impunity, making it difficult to protect products and profits. Resources to create products or services are increasingly difficult to secure. It is surely a different environment in which to do business.

Therefore, we need to adapt how we do business, how we present ourselves to the market and how we organize to serve the market, just like the military has had to adjust to venues like Afghanistan.

The purpose of this book is to provide the frameworks for designing our businesses to fit the new marketplace. It provides the basic rules and options for strategic activities and also provides clear guidelines for the organizations and cultures we need to be successful in this new environment.

In our societies, companies have a basic task: to be competitively successful, to *Sync & Swim* in this quickly evolving business environment. It is critical that a company is able to put itself into the business world so that it can "earn a living." That living is fueled by the margins that demonstrate the value provided in a commercial or nonprofit marketplace.

The design not only includes the layout of paths of activity that need to take place in order to "engage in commerce" but also includes, in human systems terms, the kind of culture and environment that best supports the activity. This becomes very apparent when the activity is about economic *competition and all organizations compete for the resources needed to survive.*

This book is about competitive design—that is, engaging in the competitive world using the appropriate strategies for the kind of competition that takes place. Understanding the major types of competition now becomes the new science. The results provide us with the building blocks for the kind of organization and leadership best fitted to engage in the kind of competition one expects in that environment.

The process of understanding these new conditions leads us to establish two kinds of related activities: First, discovering the types of competitive markets in which companies and nonprofits do business and learning just how companies need to act if they are to succeed in that environment. Second, in order to survive in that marketplace, it is critical to build organizations that fit, organizations that have the kind of design that is best suited for working in the type of competitive dynamic that characterizes each kind of market space.

The basic building blocks of this book are simple in form. You will have no trouble recognizing the four market environments that will be covered, and you will recognize the four basic organizational designs used to support business in these environments.

What will intrigue you, as it has me over the last twenty years, is the number of companies and organizations that are not in sync with their competitive environments and are thus swimming with at least one hand tied behind their back.

We will spend some time making sure we all have a similar knowledge of the four competitive market environments and how each works, and we will become familiar with the kinds of organizations that are a fit for those conditions. *But the most interesting part should be developing the ability to see where a company does not understand or respond to the competitive situation appropriately or where a company has an organization that is very different from what would work best for the kind of competition in which it is engaged.*

I think you will find this rather prevalent, which is alarming to those of us who are dedicated to helping companies be successful enterprises.

These are very different kinds of business models, and they have rules connected to them, many of which are just taken for granted or unknown by many in a company. It would seem important, for example, that the marketing and sales departments, at least, are keenly aware of the basic competitive rules that govern how competition takes place in their market.

As a business enters or exists already in a market space, what are the rules that govern the way anyone in that space endures and possibly becomes successful?

It is also a personal issue, from the standpoint of the decision to work in a particular market environment. Some rule books are more to a person's liking and talents than another.

These are important issues that all managers face, or should face, wherever they exist in any organization.

If I am developing a new business in a known market with similar products to others, how does that affect the way I plan to do business? And how is that different from a new product that will affect the business itself over time and change it into something else?

What kinds of strategies have the best chance of success in my kind of competitive market, regardless of industry? If I design my business model similarly to someone in a completely different competitive market, what should I expect?

Issues of Organization

At the same time, organizations need to be designed to fit in a particular competitive market. I might like working in the auto industry, but is that the same at Mercedes and at Ford? What is truly different about those environments, or is that just a company preference about the way business is done?

What are the rules that are followed, probably instinctively in most cases, for designing the way a company will function? Henry Ford invented new rules for making cars and setting up a means of tending to them over time. These were very different from the typical designs followed by the other car companies. But not all car companies followed him.

It is also obvious that a start-up company in Silicon Valley has a different set of rules and culture than banks on Wall Street or at the 3M company.

What we know from research on contingency theory is that *the design of the organization should fit the dynamics of the interactions that take place in that space.* A wagon train under threat forms up differently than one marching through a friendly territory. Some of this is a no-brainer, part of our survival techniques we have mastered over the years.

There are also heavy influences on the organization that come from the industry in which the organization must survive. Doctors tend to have a certain order, lawyers generally use the "partner" model, manufacturers tend to have large groups for single supervisors, professionals work differently from laborers, and on and on.

But for the leader who wants to organize to compete successfully, there is a different set of rules that if not followed, leads to disaster. Many mergers and acquisitions have ignored this fact and have often failed to meet the intended goals because of the difference in the way these rules of the market were interpreted.

The goal of this book is to get beyond the apparent rules for doing business and for designing organizations and discover what many know intuitively and others fail to understand and thus fail because of the organization flaws even when the business strategy is brilliant.

Introduction

Lawrence and Lorsch argue that if the open-system perspective is taken, rational and natural perspectives identify different organizational types, which vary because they have adapted to different types of environments. The more homogeneous and stable the environment, the more formalized and hierarchical the form. Their view is ecological—those organizations that can best adapt to the environment will survive. They see the rational system coming first because environments were initially stable and are becoming increasingly more volatile.

P. Lawrence and J. Lorsch, "Differentiation and Integration in Complex Organizations," Administrative Science Quarterly 12 (1967), 1–30.

Much of my professional life has been spent figuring out why some organizations work and others do not. Or why some people seem to easily understand business conditions and others do not. Or why things that are not supposed to work sometimes actually work—or the opposite, why some things that should work don't.

I discovered that if I focused on understanding the conflicting dynamics that are being played out in the process, I could gain a major understanding of the system and how to improve it.

For example, in the early 1980s, I witnessed a massive change in the lives of the managers with whom I was working at the 3M company. My role was to help divisions, infrastructures, departments, and many other kinds of groups develop a mission and the processes needed to be successful doing what they were charged to do.

3M managers were very concerned with two things that kept coming up in their conversations with me: first, *that they and their departments were being asked to do nearly twice what they had been expected to do just a few years before and with less than half the staff.*

At first, it seemed like this was the normal complaint coming from managers under pressure. But it became so pervasive that I began to listen more carefully to determine whether it was true, and if so, why was it happening?

If it were true, the company was going through a new development stage and everyone needed to be able to cope with this new circumstance.

Obviously, it was true, and it was being brought on by market changes that surrounded all the business. There were two changes occurring at the same time that we needed to pay attention to: we were becoming a truly globalized company with profit centers replacing sales centers, and we were now competing directly with producers who offered prices significantly less than ours and who were still very profitable. Furthermore, global competition was surpassing us significantly in terms of speed, quality, and satisfaction.

These were not changes that could be overcome by simply redesigning processes for speed and accuracy. This meant that the world was doing the basic tasks of the system much differently, much better and faster. The world had changed, and we were out of step. As an example, 3M produced videotapes for twelve dollars at that time, and suddenly, Japanese firms were selling them for five dollars. It took us a couple of years to understand that they were actually making a profit at that price.

We discovered that they looked at speed and quality very differently than we did and that if we wanted to compete with them, many things had to change in our view of the business and the kind of organizations we fostered to do the business of the company.

These two dynamics, complexity and increased competition (less margins), were the new dynamics, and all parts of the company needed to pay attention to them and design business plans and their organizations and processes around them.

In the early 1990s, governments in Europe determined that they would lower their reimbursement of pharmaceutical expenditures by 20–30 percent. This was a severe blow to several of the large companies that supplied products there. It was imperative that something needed to be done very differently if pharmaceutical companies were to survive in Europe in the long term.

From these two dynamics, the ideas of this book gradually took shape.

The basic structure of the competitive business was being affected, and unless we could get to those basic elements, we would not be able to adjust sufficiently to survive as the kind of force in the world that we had become accustomed to.

It is now clear that other businesses are similarly confronted. The broker-dealer marketplace is threatened both by significant regulation and transparency. Transactions for which they were essential are more and more possible through technology.

By determining the basic dynamics that affect these competitive businesses that were under stress from their environment, I have developed a process to examine all competitive environments to understand how these dynamics get played out in the marketplace, under stress or not.

The reality in today's world is that most businesses are under stress soon after they are created. The underlying dynamic is that the competitive marketplace eventually is more interested in the demise of the institution rather than in its continuance.

This is not the business gospel according to Jack Tesmer. It is an attempt to figure out the basic dynamics in both the places where we do business (the market) and the way we put people and processes together to successfully serve that market (the organization). These dynamics are inextricably tied together. This book explores the implications of this basic union on the rules for serving the market and the ways people create systems to serve it.

You may disagree with much of what I say, but you will definitely go away with at least one new major construct to use in running a profit or nonprofit organization. This will, in fact, mean that you will never look at the business in the same way again. You will now have access to some basic dynamics that control the business and the organizational response.

If that does not happen, let me know.

PART ONE

The Fascinating Dynamics of the Competitive Market

The competitive marketplace has a logic and set of dynamics that govern the way economic enterprises engage in the market of their choice, whether that is for profit or not for profit. In turbulent circumstances especially, understanding the market's dynamics is absolutely critical to guiding a business toward survival and success. Furthermore, all companies need to form their organizations to fit the kind of market dynamics that they experience. Most strategic processes assume that management knows about and understands the basic competitive dynamics at work. We have found this often not true, especially in small- to medium-sized companies. At the very least, there is seldom agreement among management on the nature of the competitive environment in which the company engages. There does not seem to be a model or discussion that informs the average management about the basic dynamics that affect the competitive circumstances in which business is done.

Furthermore, in an age when very disruptive companies and products seem to surface such as Amazon, Facebook, and Twitter, which challenge many business models, it is increasingly important that we understand the impact of these competitive businesses on our markets and be able to find competitive counterparts to challenge their dominance.

Not too long ago, Microsoft was the dominant force in business computing. Today that brand is being confronted from all over the world, and Apple, which was a niche player, has become dominant along with companies from Korea and many other countries with some of their products.

Understanding where these companies compete in the market is important to survive along with them, but they also are harbingers of what is to happen in our own situation. A good example is what has happened in the printing business. As digital information becomes increasingly available, the printed word is finding a new and different position in the marketplace. The daily newspaper has had to reinvent itself, for example. The question that comes to mind is whether owners and managers in the field anticipated the type of competitive changes that have taken place and what that means for their enterprises.

Sync & Swim is meant to help fill that gap, to provide a map on which all these companies can be positioned and understood for what is actually occurring now and what will probably happen to them in the near future. Finding our position on that map can help us be ready for the future, understand the implications of competitive activities that take place, and develop a position that has sustainability.

In order to understand these positions, we need to see the market in a different manner, realizing that all organizations should be formed to fit the environment in which they are trying to be successful. This new vision of the competitive market at work should inform us where we are positioned in it and give us the ability to predict where we will end up if we do nothing to change the trajectory.

We see many efforts to determine the best in class leadership or organization design, but these efforts are not always successful. In this very diverse universe of businesses, it is not possible and probably not useful to create a "perfect scenario" with an idealized organizational type. With the many competitive environments that have always been there and that are emerging, there is no place for a "one size fits all" as regards the strategic direction or the organization's culture and structure.

We believe there are some principles and dynamics that play themselves out continuously as markets evolve and encounter major periods of instability. The net effect of the recent recession, for example, is the acceleration of product and service commoditization. The pressures in the highly differentiated world were just too great to hold back this predictable force.

Sync & Swim is meant to inform management of these basic dynamics and use them to understand and plan with these in mind, much like the coach does in preparing for a *game*. Strategy becomes the *game plan* that uses the market's dynamics in constructing the development of the business.

Sync & Swim provides a view of the market where competitive business takes place, based on three practical concepts:

- First, it is only through a cogent and sober analysis of the dynamics in the kind of competitive market served that any organization can learn how to survive and succeed in it. This is especially true for any company that previously operated in one type of market environment but that, over time, has found itself pushed into another.

- Second, what we call the market is actually four separate but interactive market environments: what we will call *the Kingdom, the Battleground, the Jungle, and the Frontier.* Each environment has its own unique dynamics, which create a self-organizing structure with its own rules, requirements, players, and style of competition. Most managers in the trenches have an immediate and intuitive recognition of these different market environments, usually from their names alone.

- Third, just as most products and services need to be designed around customer requirements and desires, *a successful company needs to be organized around the dynamics of the market environment in which it seeks to compete.* It is not enough to simply design a marketing strategy around your market; *your entire organization itself must have a structure, a culture, and a set of internal systems that suit its particular market environment.*

Organizations, of course, differ greatly from one another and always have. Companies, for example, differ according to the product or service they provide, like lawyers, university faculties, and manufacturing and service companies. Nevertheless, over the past two decades, we have discovered some clear, identifiable organizational types that all or most companies fit in to. Each different type is particularly well suited to one of the four market environments.

At the heart of this volume are two simple and connected principles:

1. Every organization is attempting to find and use resources, like capital and people, to survive in our competitive environment.

Therefore, *management needs to understand the dynamics of the competing environment in order to be successful in it.*

2. When an organization has the appropriate organizational structure for its market environment, *a synergy is created that deeply supports and empowers the organization, its management, and its workforce.*

Archetypes

In this book, I will name and refer to *archetypes* of markets and organizations. These are used to designate groups that share similar circumstances and dynamics and therefore allow us to understand the conditions of operating and the requirements of organization.

Understanding the nature of each type of market and each type of organization will be the most critical part of guiding/coaching the business and the organization that serves it in a competent manner, especially in the present environment of great *volatility, uncertainty, complexity, and ambiguity.*

There are four market archetypes:

- **Frontiers, Jungles, Battlegrounds, and Kingdoms**—each has its own distinct needs, driving forces, and strategies for success.

There are also four organizational archetypes:

- **Pioneers, Hunters, Warriors, and Rulers**—each should be designed and run according to the needs and demands of the particular type of market it serves.

It is our experience, over the last twenty years of using the archetypes to describe the markets that are crucial to a company's success, that there is usually a good deal of disagreement concerning the market archetype served by the company among the top management team! The effect on common decisions and leadership is significant, to say the least.

Sync & Swim will help you to understand the dynamics of these archetypes and how your organization fits within them. This is the beginning of strategy and needs to precede and inform all strategic thinking and planning! *This is also the basis for creating alignment between those who create and manage strategic initiatives.*

What You Will Find in the Next Chapters

In the opening chapters of this book, you'll be introduced to the four competitive market environments that have become apparent as we get deeper into the twenty-first century as well as to the organizational archetypes that can operate most profitably in each one.

You will then learn about and try using a sample of a unique assessment tool to identify what type of market environment your own organization needs to be operating in, as well as the archetypal structure upon which it is currently built.

There are four parts to this identification:

1. *Determining and getting agreement on the present market position of the business and its potential*
2. *Determining and getting agreement on the strategic position that is desirable for the product or service*
3. *Determining the appropriateness of the organizational structure and culture for serving these markets*
4. *Determining what needs to change in that pattern and practice*

If your company and your market are not well suited for one another, then something needs to change. This may mean changing your organization's products, services, or markets. More than likely, however, there will need to be a transformation of the organization itself so that it takes on the general structure of the archetype that is best suited for its market environment.

The third part of this book will help you discover what options you have for changing your organization's business strategy, structure, and culture. It will offer specific guidance for moving from one market to another and examine the issues and opportunities that are likely to appear. Finally, it will look closely at some ways to more carefully analyze your own organization and support the needed steps toward change.

This book's key concepts have been field tested and refined for over two decades in organizations in the United States and Europe and in many evolving market environments. These concepts and tools can transform the way your organization thinks of itself, treats its customers and employees, and competes in its marketplace.

What's the bottom line of reading this book and putting its concepts into practice? A company that is saner, better run, more responsive to its market, and more competitive and profitable.

In case you have doubts about the relevance of the discussions in which you are about to participate, just ask yourself, "What happened to the following businesses that were at one time considered highly successful?"

- IBM pre-1990 was principally a hardware manufacturer of large computer equipment and produced high-end products for businesses at significant prices. The market changed quickly as information storage advanced in technology, and IBM is now mainly a software and systems services company.
- K-Mart, Sears, and eventually, Penney's were the standard in merchandising to the everyday purchaser of clothing, tools, and household items. Amazon has changed the purchasing experience completely, and these companies are struggling.
- The dot-coms in 2000 proved to be too exotic and impractical to sustain themselves, and investors left them in droves.
- Hewlett-Packard manufactured printing and accessories for all kinds of computers, with a major emphasis on the ink necessary to print and service people who got their information from the typed page. Today, people carry around that information on phones and tablets and expect it to be stored in the cloud.
- Project management consulting firms have been important for servicing installations of information systems in businesses. As these systems have improved, the need for temporary expert help has decreased significantly.
- Blackberry and Nokia were at one time the primary brands for handheld devices. They have been replaced by the iPhone and Android phones almost completely as innovations on these devices have made the old forms obsolete.

- 3M was the leader in recording technology, which was reflected by the twelve-to-fifteen-dollar price in the early 1980s, until several Japanese firms suddenly offered the equivalent product for one-third that price, and the product also became obsolete.
- SuperValue, a large distributor of grocery goods in the United States, after attempting to compete directly with Walmart and Target, who began selling groceries and using their considerable transportation capacity, had to redefine their purpose and offerings, resulting in a much smaller operation.

All these companies were subjected to significant competitive market forces that could have been forecast and were forecast in some instances. The issue is whether there were archetypical understandings that would have proven useful in weathering the market forces with which they were dealing. In some cases, the internal disagreements over the nature of the market were very significant and have yet to be resolved.

The following chapters should provide ideas why these companies and companies like your own, as well as your competitors', were or are under such pressure to adapt and how well they survived the crisis.

Turn the page and you'll begin learning how to help create the transformations needed in your organization to be successful in the changing economy and to help you, as a manager or coach, guide your business through the archetype markets using your strategies to achieve a successful outcome.

CHAPTER ONE

Types of Competitive Markets

What happens when a broker-dealer finance company finds that all the principles are in their sixties and the industry is in the midst of consolidation, the regulatory environment has become tighter, and due to technology advances, information on investment options is available to everyone?

It is clearly time to redirect the business. The development of a business-survival strategy should begin with a clear understanding of the competitive environment in which business will occur. That usually contentious environment dictates the rules and tactics that will be successful in establishing a presence and gaining customers. Strategy, by definition, is about competing, and for this reason, we need to understand the competitive dynamics that shape and define various kinds of market environments.

The dynamics of a process can usually be visualized by determining the tensions that are being worked out consistently in that process. In the case of competition that occurs in the marketplace, two tensions that are most consistently at play are about the level of risk or reward (usually measured by the level of margins that can be expected or the amount of resources one side has over the other) that is involved and the amount of control and certainty that exists in the competitive situation. These two dimensions exist in all competitive environments, whether that is in the profit or the nonprofit environment. To understand the interplay between these, we can build a four-block matrix that illustrates at least four different kinds of competition. Alex Lowy and Phil Hood in *The Power of the 2 × 2 Matrix* describe this process and the many uses this kind of model has in understanding the dynamics of common situations. A similar matrix will be used to illustrate the dynamics that affect the organization and help determine the kinds of organizational response that fits in each of the four situations.

There is another set of rules that entrepreneurs must be aware of. They come from the kind of industry in which business is done. Doing business in the clothing industry is vastly different from selling automobiles, for example. *This book will not focus on these industry-specific ways of doing business.* We will look particularly at the kinds of issues that mostly affect the sustainability of the enterprise—that is, what the competitive rules and dynamics that generally apply to all businesses are.

In this chapter, we will identify four different but connected archetypes that comprise the options for choosing the kind of competitive conditions that best fit the business in which we engage. This now becomes the "playing field" in which management positions the business and attempts various strategies to attain success.

The Four Competitive Market Archetypes

Each of today's organizations operates in one or more of four distinctly different competitive market environments: the *Kingdom*, the *Battleground*, the *Jungle*, and the *Frontier*. The following figure presents a view of the four and will be used throughout the book as a visual map in determining the market served and the strategies that are most appropriate in the position an enterprise finds itself.

This will eventually be one of two matrices a person can use to navigate the competitive environment in which he or she does business.

First, let's describe the characteristics of each of these competitive positions. As you read through the book, you will gain more and more information about these positions and expectations that are encountered in each. The vertical axis represents the kind of margins that are prevalent in your situation. Margins might be rather large, for example, because you have a product that has a patent and is very much in demand. Or the margins could be quite slim because the product is a commodity. Coca-Cola and Pepsi or the major beer companies or sneaker manufacturers essentially live with lower margins unless they can find some feature that can be added to increase the demand, but it still essentially is a commodity.

On the horizontal axis, we measure the amount of predictability and control a company has over the market, its future, variations in the market, etc. New products and highly competitive products are in this condition.

More will be said about these markets, but now you have the basics of the rationale for separating out the four major market types. The following figure illustrates these markets. Each of these markets will be described more fully beginning after figure 1.

Strategic Market Archetypes

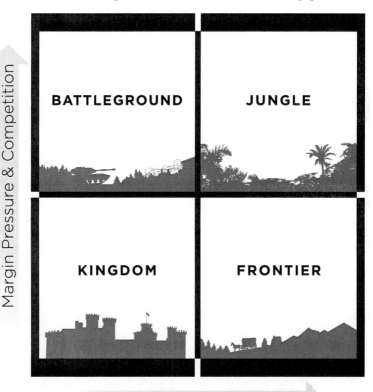

Kingdom

Kingdom markets are those served by companies that have achieved a controlling position in the market. That may come from attributes of the product (think Apple products) or because they have control of the distribution chain or they have a patent on the product. They have the least competition and market difficulty as long as they control their borders.

Companies that have operated successfully in a Kingdom dominate and rule their part of the market. They have the luxury of producing what *they* believe is valuable—first to themselves then to their customers. Of course, they can easily get too independent of customer desires. In the best case, they are able to stay ahead of the customer and, in fact, drive customer desires, as Apple certainly does.

Pharmaceutical companies tend to have product lines in the Kingdom as long as the patent holds out. When generic manufacturers begin to enter the market as the patent runs its course, that product line leaves the Kingdom. Companies that want to remain in the Kingdom need to continually upgrade their offerings so that others cannot duplicate or threaten them. Dominating the market is a key activity of companies that want to remain in this market.

Typically, these companies can win out over new competitors because their high margins provide them with enough resources to dominate the market. Anyone attempting to gain entry is quickly brushed aside through huge advertising campaigns, litigation on patents, large temporary price drops on competing products, and other expensive but highly effective tactics.

In a Kingdom market, customers have a clear need for the industry's products and services; indeed, demand often outstrips supply. Obviously, some Kingdom companies have created much of that demand by focusing on some attribute that customers value highly. Customers (as well as just about everyone in the supply chain) are more concerned with back orders than with quality. Microsoft, until lately, has been notorious about expecting customers to detect problems in the software during the launching period.

Products and technologies cannot be replicated and are distinct enough to not be able to be duplicated, making conditions stable and predictable. Think 3M Post-it Notes.

Battleground

A Battleground environment is very competitive, mainly with a few large producers. Products and services marketed in this environment are familiar and well understood—e.g., cola, running shoes, photocopiers, air travel, aggregates. A few large players tend to dominate and compete vigorously, making their profit through volume.

These products are usually referred to as *commodities*. Customers expect steadily increasing quality, and the focus is on delivering products and services to as many customers as possible, as quickly and cheaply as possible. Companies that serve this market are always concerned with their number of points of distribution (PODs). Increase these and you increase sales; control these sufficiently and you control price and distribution. In a Battleground environment, companies thus fight two battles: a battle of numbers and a battle for the minds of consumers.

This is the market of consolidation, where only size and control will merit enough business to be profitable. The major airlines and banks are good examples.

Most new products—as they become widely known, accepted, and used—eventually drift into this environment. As a product becomes simpler to make and easier to get to market, the players in the industry begin to consolidate in the struggle to profitably produce it.

Jungle

Jungle markets combine two of the most difficult marketing situations. On the one hand, margins are under considerable pressure. On the other, there is a great deal of difficulty in positioning, monitoring, and controlling products or services.

Most players in this market have products that came out of the Frontier and are now being sorted out by the market. What was previously protected by patents may now be in competition with a new "me too" product, which skirts the patent through the clever use of technology. Ultimately, winners will emerge and losers will disappear, and consolidation will take the market into the Battleground. The market is highly influenced by the easy-entry potential for anyone who wants to duplicate or challenge a product.

Products and services in a Jungle market are expected to compete on both price and accommodation or service. This creates both complexity and difficulty in production and distribution. Meanwhile, conditions keep changing rapidly and are influenced by multiple outside forces.

The dynamics in this market are conditioned around doing "more for less" in a continuous spiral toward doing "everything for nothing."

These companies tend to be small- to medium-sized and are in highly competitive businesses. Many service companies are in this market, along with specialty manufacturing, contractual engineering, and construction. It is a relatively easy market to enter, so we see many smaller businesses here.

Frontier

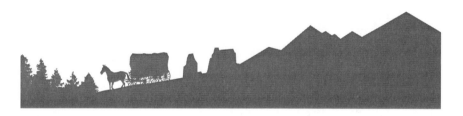

Most of the products and services in this market environment are new ones. A significant portion of these create their own new market niches and, in some cases, entirely new industries. Margins tend to be significant, but markets are often difficult to enter and serve. The two primary difficulties are (1) introducing new products or services into existing distribution channels (or, sometimes, creating new ones), and (2) managing the costs and technical complexity of new product development.

Their seems to be at least two different ways to exist in this market: either invest significantly to quickly move into the Kingdom or "make a little, sell a little" to find the key market advantages but end up in the Jungle because of the time it takes to gain acceptance and use by a sufficient number of customers that can make it sustainable.

In order to survive the entry process, companies need to develop significant resources, normally through high margins. Because the products or services are new, information about them is not readily available. This essentially forces a company to invest heavily in advertising.

Doing business in a Frontier environment is often unpredictable, risky, and opportunistic. Nevertheless, some firms—the pharmaceutical company Merck, for example—have developed very successful new product launch processes that get them into markets ahead of competitors and allow them to acquire more than adequate margins quite quickly.

Here is a bird's-eye view of all those interactive market environments.

Market Environments

High

	WARRIORS	HUNTERS

Level of Competition

WARRIORS	HUNTERS
• Restricted Margins • Few Serious Competitors • Predictable and Stable • Clear & Obvious Market Structure	• Constricting Margins • Many Serious Competitors • Very Turbulent • Complex & Ambiguous Business Environment
RULERS	**PIONEERS**
• Acceptable Margins • No Significant Competition • A Demand Market • Predictable and Stable Market • Clear & Obvious Market Structure	• Above-average Margins • A New Market • Turbulent • Complex & Ambiguous Business Environment

Low   **Degree of Complexity & Unpredictability**   High

In Kingdom markets, one or two companies dominate; in Jungles, multiple companies contest vigorously for every percentage point of market share. In Frontiers, companies open new markets; in Battlegrounds, they close them.

Determining the True Position of a Business in Each Market

The grid that follows is useful in demonstrating the dynamic environment in which companies find themselves. It is useful to break down the position of a company within whichever market it exists.

Market/Organization Profile

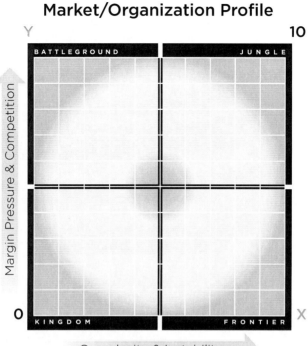

Y   10

BATTLEGROUND   **JUNGLE**

Margin Pressure & Competition

KINGDOM   **FRONTIER**

0   X

Complexity & Instability
(unpredictability)

Companies, or general product lines, do business in one of the four markets. Using a structured examination, we will be able to identify which market is served as well *as the specific position in that market.* This position will tell us just how the market's dynamics are affecting the company, or, how well the company is managing the dynamics that are in play in that part of the market.

Thus, a Jungle market has four potential positions available with it. These can be further articulated so that we have a more precise understanding of just how the market's dynamics are affecting the company.

Therefore, a company can find itself in a position in the upper right part of the Jungle market, and that has a definite implication. Through a series of questions that you will become more familiar with in the next chapters, we will be able to pinpoint a position in the marketplace that not only indicates in which of the four markets you think you are doing business *but also how well you are doing business in that market and what some of the major issues you are dealing with are.*

In the upper right corner of the Jungle market, you would be experiencing significant pressure on margins, along with a desperate scramble to meet the changing and unpredictable needs that come with a highly competitive environment. In that position, we can predict that the business is not sustainable and is ripe for dissolution or consolidation, for example.

Generally, we say that anything above a diagonal line dividing the market from upper left to lower right is being threatened with serious concerns about sustainability. Other things can be derived from that position, and we will say more about this as we move through the rest of the book.

Suffice it to say at this time that the most desirable position in each of the markets is near the center of the grid. In each market, that means something different.

Through the use of a questionaire, we will be able to ascertain a fairly accurate position that reflects the situation for each company that takes an assessment. That is described in the next chapter.

It is important to point out that this model becomes useful when used to find out the present position in a particular market, to understand the pressures on that position, and to determine solutions to maintaining it or achieving a more sustainable position.

Chapter Two

Market Dynamics

The dynamics in organizations and markets are the results of tensions and forces that are active in the marketplace. The major tension is between the interests of competitors that get reflected in the competitive actions that occur between them. It is about controlling the marketplace so that some advantage is created. Securing advantage generally means that one of the competitors is able to respond more adequately to demand and can find ways to secure or increase margins needed to have a successful business, a struggle to create resources to produce or market products and deliver a profit.

All businesses are seeking resources in the form of a price for products and services, which pays for the costs of doing business and leaves a margin for use in growing the company and paying the various stakeholders. The greater the margin, the greater the ability of the company to market products in that market where margins are significant. This is the first and the most important dynamic.

We often hear that business is all about making money. Even though that may sound Machiavellian, it is certainly true that all businesses, profit and nonprofit, are seeking resources that allow the institution to continue to exist. That struggle creates a dynamic that is affecting all businesses constantly. Depending on the niche served, we must follow a unique strategic style if the company is to survive, succeed, and excel. In short, what will work for Coca-Cola will spell disaster for Amazon. com, and vice versa. This competitive struggle is inevitable in all the four markets but has a different form in each. These are represented by the following figure. If allowed to exist without competing forces, each market will eventually drive a business into extinction.

Market Dynamics

BATTLEGROUND	JUNGLE
LESS FOR LESS	MORE FOR LESS
MORE FOR MORE	LESS FOR MORE
KINGDOM	FRONTIER

Every business in each of these markets faces these same dynamics, which, if not countered by a powerful strategy, will drive the business out of that market. However, the act of management and strategy is to work against this tide, to attempt to slow it down, so that the enterprise can satisfy the needs of the stakeholders.

In the Jungle, the driver is to do more and more for less and less as competitors enter the market and attempt to win customers. If kept unchecked, they do everything for nothing. Obviously, things happen before that happens; like consolidations, businesses give up and leave, or a counterforce of some kind drives the business back toward the center.

Market Dynamics

In each of the markets, the dynamic driver behaves a little differently: In the Jungle, we do more and more for less and less; in the Battleground, *we do less for less*, meaning we strip the product or service to as essential an attribute as we can and compete on price. In the Kingdom, we attempt to produce more and charge more until a new competitor comes by and challenges us in the marketplace. This happened to 3M in the '80s when they were producing videotapes for fifteen dollars each and the Japanese companies like Sony suddenly offered them on the shelf for five dollars. This was a top product line for 3M, and they thought the Japanese could not make any profit on the five-dollar price. It took them two years to find out differently. 3M had sunk into the lower corner of the Kingdom and had become vulnerable. In the Frontier, we are pressured to try to get more and more for our products and services but include less and less in the offering.

Management's role is to develop ways of countering those dynamic drivers. In the Jungle, we innovate to reduce the slippage in price; in the Battleground, we add small attributes to the product that seem like major changes but retains the price; in the Kingdom, we attempt to meet some additional needs of the customer that will not be a major cost; and in the Frontier, we try to find ways of adapting the offering to the customer's interests so that they are willing to pay the costs.

Another dynamic is the struggle to control the destiny of the enterprise and all that is part of it. We gain control by the amount of knowledge and influence we have on markets that we serve. The more of the supply chain we control, the more we can ensure that the margins will be sufficient for the company to do what it wants to do. The more we control, the more influence we have in setting and collecting abundant resources or profit margins. The struggle to gain resources is related to the struggle to develop control of all the processes that affect the product sale.

The more control we have of the present and future of the business activity, the more potential we have for doing business in the Kingdom.

The following figure illustrates these dynamics.

Market Dynamics

Let's look at these dynamics in more detail, one market environment at a time.

Kingdoms and Dominated Markets

Here the dynamics are set up by the struggle to keep margins at a high enough level to provide all the rewards expected by all company stakeholders. In companies that operate successfully in Kingdom markets, we often hear the words "maintaining traditional growth and profit percentages." Because margins are significant, demand is high, and the company controls a large portion of market share, the stakes are high for companies that dominate. Power is often exercised by purchasing successful (or new) competitors. Generally, large margins are critical to the overall system in order to keep all divisions at a high level and to afford significant investments in new proprietary products, which will fetch significant margins that keep the new products coming. We often think they have one foot in the Kingdom and one in the Frontier.

Battlegrounds and Closed Markets

Businesses that compete in a Battleground environment eventually go through consolidation into a few very powerful players who share most or all the market. The most important dynamic here is that this market is essentially closed to all other comers. Anyone trying to get in will be considered a much lesser or niche player, and the handful of giant competitors will determine how much of a dent is made in their customer base. If that portion becomes too prominent for comfort, they will attempt to purchase it.

Entrance into Battleground markets is almost impossible. It can be done—the Fox network is one such success—but only with the expenditure of enormous financial or political capital. The cost of developing the many required points of distribution is usually so great that few attempt to enter in a significant way.

In many Battleground markets, margins become very small as the battle wears on. The principal criterion for success thus often becomes increased volume.

Jungles and Contested Markets

Jungle dynamics are based on pricing and product differentiation. Because margins get gradually eaten away as competition continues, alliances of all kinds are created to maintain market share, and they are often quickly dissolved for the same reasons. The dynamics of this market are determined by the kind of competition that is prominent, which is basically defined by a continual drive of giving more product or service for less and less return in order to compete in the market.

Just when a company may think that it has secured a certain group of customers, another player may appear (often from another country) with a slightly different product or a significant price reduction.

The key word here is *turbulence*. Change may come from technology, new products, a new set of alliances, significant price cuts, government intervention, or many other sources.

Most companies begin in the Frontier and, because they are unable to secure their market or funding, end up in the Jungle. It is the result of the "make a little, sell a little" marketing process. This is, at least, a time-consuming process during which potential competitors emerge, especially if the innovation has significant value in the market.

Several years ago, one 3M vice president said that to simply survive in a Jungle market (in this case, the market for floppy disks and hardware), it was necessary to develop 100 percent new products every four years. Not surprisingly, 3M amputated that part of the company and formed a separate one called Imation. Imation created its own separate culture, one designed specifically to survive in a Jungle market.

Management's role in this market is to counteract the dynamic of more for less through innovation, marketing, and systems management.

Frontiers and Open Markets

In a Frontier market environment, products are new and unknown and have no significant customer base. Anyone can enter; there are no dues to pay and no real competitors if the product or service is truly new. Here the dynamic focuses on finding customers and becoming known and valued. This is a very different dynamic from defending territory that has already been gained. Another common focus is developing a funding base to support the development of the market. (This activity can easily become all-consuming.)

Innovativeness is the norm here. There usually is not a major effort at keeping costs down; indeed, if the field and/or product is valued by Wall Street, funds become readily available through the issuance of an IPO.

There is also a pattern to the way products move through these markets. The following figure presents some of the development issues that are experienced.

Market Evolution Dynamics

BATTLEGROUND	JUNGLE
ERRODING MARKETS	TURBULENT AND SWIFT TRANSITIONS
PREDICTABLE AND SLOW TRANSITIONS	DEVELOPING MARKETS
KINGDOM	FRONTIER

Kingdom markets evolve slowly and are therefore relatively manageable as long as there is a culture of domination. The common characteristics here are stability, constancy, predictability, power, and control. Budgeting in this environment usually means adding or subtracting a percentage of the current year's figure.

Battleground markets are always eroding. Nothing less than constant attention is necessary to keep products and services from becoming unprofitable. The most common element here is constant differentiation, which is crucial for stemming the erosion of the market. (Dishwasher soap companies add a different color ingredient and calls it *new* as differentiation.)

Jungle markets change very quickly, often on a day-to-day basis. That is the common element here. Products and services themselves may change from week to week. The emphasis by management has to be on innovation to withstand the drive toward a commodity, which eventually will happen, but the longer it can be subverted by new ideas and products, the longer the product will stay in the Jungle and live by a different set of rules than if it becomes a commodity in the Battleground.

The central characteristics of *Frontier markets* are growth and invention—becoming bigger, better known, more versatile, more innovative, or just different from the competition.

Again, the most critical choice in this market is whether the product or service can become a Kingdom product or can only move toward the Jungle because it cannot be controlled from new entries in the market.

Stages in the Life of a Product

Yet another crucial dynamic involves the life of each particular product or service and, in some cases, groups of products or services. Each starts out in the Frontier as something new to the world and, thus, more or less proprietary. As it becomes better known and more widely accepted, however, it turns slowly (and sometimes not so slowly) into a commodity. In other words, it has gone through the crucible of business consolidations that lead to low margins and high volume. A good example is personal computers. These were essentially new products until the late 1980s but are now commodity items with few differences between brands and may become obsolete altogether.

In some cases, this involves whole groups of products. Print publishing has been experiencing this evolution for some time. It is not yet clear what will settle out as the inhereter of the next stage of products. Newspapers have settled into another role, magazines still seem to be evolving, and print advertising has been moving to digital for some time.

Until the digital revolution product lines evolved very slowly, in many companies that had distinctive patents, they could rely on at least fifteen years of protected existence in the market. The presence of immediate information availability allows substitutes to be derived quickly. Just as soon as Apple comes out with a new iPhone, Samsung is soon there with a slightly different but comparable version to challenge Apple.

Two good examples of companies that favor proprietary products are Merck and 3M. Both organizations' products start out in the Frontier then tend to drift toward a Kingdom or a Jungle environment. The company can deal effectively with either of these outcomes—but if a product moves too far in the direction of a Battleground, it cannot support the infrastructure and is soon discarded.

In contrast, other companies clearly have a commodity atmosphere and culture. Anheuser-Busch, for example, has not brought out a new beer in years. Its products may be given a slight change in color or dryness, but the company avoids offering a significant "new to the world" beer. Anheuser-Busch simply does not have the culture to support that sort of innovation. The organization lives with numbers in the tens of millions of bottles and tens of millions of dollars; its people simply cannot be comfortable bringing on a new line with numbers in the hundreds of thousands.

Sync the quality of commodity products is similar, commodity-oriented companies engage in a battle for the lowest cost and the most shelf space, use, or visibility.

These organizations thus spend much of their marketing activity creating new points of distribution.

Commodity organizations tend to focus on the following:

- Brand management
- Low-cost suppliers
- Lean manufacturing
- Simplification of processes
- Extensive advertising
- Image development
- Shelf space tactics
- Product differentiation

- Intensive marketing
- Product extensions
- Speed of adaptation
- Standardization

In contrast, companies holding proprietary rights to their products are especially concerned with building markets. They thus tend to focus on the following:

- Customization
- Product technology
- Intensive R&D
- New product development
- Market acceptance
- Market knowledge
- Advanced manufacturing technology
- Market domination
- Speed in getting to market

The life cycle of products and services has undergone a major change over the past decades. Years ago, a product or service would be born in a Frontier setting, achieve high margins in an open market with lots of opportunity. As time went on, it typically moved rather quickly into a Kingdom market, where, with the help of easy patents, efforts were successful in dominating that market and prices and margins remained high for long periods.

A product could then be reasonably expected to remain in a Kingdom market for fifteen to twenty-five years. This would allow for many products with good margins, which would support both the Kingdom bureaucracy and any new product development. The product would eventually become a commodity as the patent wore out and other companies began to manufacture it much more cheaply. Normally, this would take long enough that the bureaucratic superstructure and new product development costs would be more than covered.

Today's normal cycle is much different. It begins in the same manner, but today, most new products and services move very quickly—often within weeks or months—into a Jungle environment. Here it is confronted with similar products, and domination is seldom attained.

As a result, margins are lower, and very quickly thereafter, many players disappear or are acquired. A handful of companies end up in a Battleground, producing the product as a commodity.

Another phenomenon is now apparent in this life cycle process. If a product is not a sure bet to capture market share and dominate right away, it works slowly toward a Jungle market. By the time it is a full-fledged product line, it has many competitors that have observed its development and found ways of competing with it.

Other products are seen to have great potential and receive considerable assistance in their start-up. Investors understand that these are future Kingdom products, so work is done immediately to hasten their development before competition develops. This calls for considerable up-front assistance and investment.

These two tracks toward maturity and beyond are shown in the next figure.

Two Very Different Product Life Cycle Paths

The implications of this are both many and immense. The most important ones are the following:

1. In Kingdom companies, new products are developed not only to provide superior revenue in the long term for the company. They are the source of higher margin potential that is used to invest in the development of more new products of superior value and innovation. Not only is this process critical to remaining in the Kingdom but it is also threatened recently by the ability of competitors to reduce the superior competitive position through new information technology. Thus the amount of investment in innovation continues to increase significantly (e.g., companies like IBM, 3M, and pharmaceuticals and medical device businesses like Medtronic and Johnson & Johnson).

2. The cost of new product development needs to be continually challenged through increasing the speed and prioritization of product ideas that have significant potential since the time in which a new product or service can produce tolerable margins has grown shorter and more new products need to come to market more quickly.

3. Much of management's strategy is focused on the need to keep products from running through the whole cycle of Frontier to Battleground too quickly.

PART TWO

Arranging the
Organization to Compete

Sync & Swim is a concept built around two sets of dynamics that are played out in the marketplace. We have discussed the first set in the first two chapters that concern the dynamics of the competitive market itself. There are forces operating in that environment that determine the conditions for successful competition, which should be mastered if anyone decides to do business.

Understanding these forces and the context created by them is very much like understanding the terrain on which a battle is to be fought or a game is to be won. As we have said, the context determines the strategy.

Now it is time to focus on the structure and culture of the organization that is needed in these various situations. The next two chapters outline the four types of organizational archetypes and discuss the various systems that help understand the dynamics internal to these organizational types.

With these four chapters, you have the background to begin assessing the companies that you know or are part of. The motive will be first to determine if their enterprise is experiencing their market successfully, is positioned appropriately in the market, and is able to set an appropriate direction for the future in it.

This is the first part of *Sync & Swim*—understanding and managing the market position so that there is a potential for success and so that we can adequately predict the future development needed in that position.

Sync & Swim is about knowing the potential of the organization to operate in that marketplace and understanding what it will take to keep a good position or develop a better one so that the organization and the market position are *in sync*.

The next two chapters will focus on the organizational dynamics. Following that, we will develop a vision of the whole process and be ready to assess markets and organizations, which will happen in part 3.

CHAPTER THREE

Organizational Archetypes

Organizational Fitness

In nature, successful organisms—whether they're sharks, orchids, or impalas—are designed to survive and thrive in their particular environments. Paradoxically, however, the same characteristics that make a creature so successful in its natural environment also restrict its ability to survive elsewhere.

The same principles hold true for businesses and markets. *There needs to be a fit between the dynamics of an organization and the market environment in which it operates.* Indeed, this fit is crucial to the company's survival. This is a central theme of this book. It is its breakthrough concept. It is the most difficult part for many organizations to accept. It runs against the experience and preferences of several parts of organizations. It is not easy to implement and is at the core of the issues surrounding what is known as organizational culture.

Furthermore, a company that has everything it needs to thrive in one market environment is likely to fail when it attempts to enter another—unless, of course, it makes a deliberate decision to adapt. However, as we have shown, *products and services mature over time and change their environment when that happens.*

An organization's fitness for its environment rarely comes about by accident. Its leaders need to have a very clear understanding of the dynamics of its markets so that it is able to respond to them deliberately and effectively.

This chapter briefly describes and analyzes the four different organizational archetypes, each one uniquely suited for one of the four basic market environments.

A simple breakdown looks like this:

Market Environment	Best-Suited Type of Organization
Kingdom	Ruler
Battleground	Warrior
Jungle	Hunter
Fontier	Pioneer

The rest of this chapter—and indeed, much of this book—will describe, compare, and differentiate these four organizational archetypes in a variety of ways.

Four Organizational Ways of Life

The four organizational archetypes—Rulers, Warriors, Hunters, and Pioneers—can be compared and differentiated in a wide variety of ways. Initially, however, they can be identified by

1. how open they are to what is happening with their markets or customers, including how open management is to hearing the feedback and making use of it, and
2. how collectively they operate, that is, how much interaction is seen as expected and/or necessary to get the work done.

Markets are constantly changing either in subtle or significant ways. Some organizations need to be very attentive to all the activities and changes that are going on with their market so that they can constantly adapt in ways that make them desirable to their customers. Others are confident that their practices, products, and services will be accepted and will fit into the marketplace without adaptation since they have significant control, have set the rules and margins, and have assured that the demand is so great and steady that there is no real need to be very attentive.

The following figure shows how these two dynamics are similar to the market forces in the previous chapters. On the vertical axis, we show *the variations of organizations that have significant attention to the external conditions in which they operate, with the intention of constantly adjusting internally to what is happening externally, to the opposite stance in which organizations are more or less impervious to external changes and conditions and write the rules based more on their needs than on those of the market.*

For example, pharmaceutical companies, as long as they control the patent, will tend to charge prices that, to their way of thinking, help them to recover the costs of innovation and marketing that go along with bringing new drugs to market, whether these prices are acceptable or not.

On the horizontal axis, we position the dynamic of *interaction needed to get things to work.* Some companies rely only on the independent work of individuals in accomplishing tasks. Production lines are usually very individualistic, with each worker given a particular discreet task and not much, if any, interaction needed to accomplish the task.

(This kind of organizing usually creates the need for some bureaucratic management to make sure that large tasks get accomplished. It is not unusual in these companies to find that little dynasties are created by bureaucratic managers who make certain that things happen in the manner they feel must take place.)

On the other hand, there are companies that operate in just the opposite manner, where tasks are not clear and people need to find ways to work together to get difficult things to happen. The role of the manager in these cases is to make sure that the members have all they need to work together to accomplish tasks. These situations are most useful where there is ambiguity and uncertainty surrounding the work to be done.

These two dynamics intertwine to form the various types of organizational responses we see in the marketplace. They form a four-block model similar to the one we have used for the marketplace, and upon closer examination, you can see that the kinds of combinations that are formed in this diagram are symbiotic with the market matrix. That is, each of the four types of organization relates to the market type in the same part of the matrix.

Strategic Organizational Archetypes

The Organization Matrix

Thus we come across the central theme of this book—that each market has a typical kind of organization appropriate to its dynamics. If you are going to serve the Jungle market, then it is most appropriate that you have an organization that is highly attentive to the outside market and very good at working synergistically. That makes sense since *from experience, we can all see that the Jungle market, with its massive amounts of competitive behavior emanating from the easy entrance of competition, is presenting the biggest challenges to organizational life and therefore should merit the largest challenge in terms of synergistic human behavior.*

Let's drill down another level and look more deeply and specifically at the characteristics of each of the four organizational archetypes.

Rulers

In order to respond to a Kingdom market environment, Rulers need to concentrate on fulfilling whatever demands are driving the market. Minimal external customer data are needed, except those that determine delivery goals. Little information about competitors is required, except when there are serious attempts to encroach on the market.

In short, a Ruler can function well almost entirely on internal ideas. The big issue is usually figuring out ways to cope with demand. Since the demand is so great, quality usually gets improved slowly whenever sufficient time and resources are available. Many problems are simply solved financially—e.g., by hiring the most talented people, buying up competitors, etc. (Microsoft is notorious for expecting its customers to find the glitches in a new operating system).

The central dynamic of this kind of organization is that without attention, management practices and organizational structures become less and less relevant and focused. They are more and more captured by their own goals and interests.

Examples: Microsoft, Apple, Medtronic, Boeing, Merck

Warriors

In order to respond effectively in a Battleground market environment, Warriors need to concentrate on (1) increasing demand for their products or services and (2) expanding and improving their distribution. Since margins tend to continually erode, Warriors need to be ever vigilant for new ways to find market openings and make new inroads. In part, this means being open to ideas from outside the organization about how to expand the market. This often means borrowing ideas and strategies from competitors.

People in a Warrior organization normally can and should operate independently. There is a very significant exception, however: sales projects are usually huge, demanding great coordination over vast geographical distances. These can succeed only through very strong management, which draws people together to carry out a common strategy. Such concerted action requires a great deal of planning and organization. People in these kinds of organizations tend to react well to these initiatives. They are very experienced in doing what management wants done, without the need to make it understandable and acceptable.

Examples: Coca-Cola and Pepsi, Burger King and McDonald's, Target and Walmart, and Procter & Gamble, Bristol-Myers, Colgate-Palmolive, Budweiser, and Miller High Life

Hunters

In order to respond to a Jungle market environment, Hunters need to be successful at contradictory, and seemingly impossible, tasks—meeting customer expectations superbly while managing constantly shrinking margins. Alertness to moves by competitors and the ability to counter them are absolutely crucial.

Hunters normally need an organizational structure that focuses the attention of everyone on the market. This structure must also be able to make internal adaptations very quickly. In practice, this usually requires a highly interdependent culture and the same kind of sharing of information and effort that is seen in start-up organizations. There needs to be a simultaneous emphasis on keeping quality up and internal costs down.

These organizations must have mechanisms in place to monitor market movements carefully, accurately, and in a timely fashion. This information then must be made quickly and widely available throughout the organization.

To really exercise control and influence in this market, it is necessary to focus the attention of the whole system on the market by developing business units that concentrate on segments or niches that have promise and then creating the kind of relationships that allow for significant influence to be exercised on key aspects of these customer groups.

These units then become Hunters, who exploit the opportunities that they search out and develop. The results of the products and services are then used to continue the customer relationship and improve delivery as well as expand the coverage. This is active marketing that is supplemented by the passive activities as advertising and media penetration.

Examples: financial services, specialty manufacturing, physician specialists, engineering firms, consulting groups, publishing firms

Pioneers

Pioneer organizations must concentrate on developing new products and finding ways of getting them accepted into the market in a significant way. This is a highly unpredictable and complex task, especially when it involves displacing a competitor's product. The process needs to be driven by some internal function, normally research and development, and the entire system and culture need to be structured around that function.

People who work for Pioneer organizations need to be able to act highly interdependently, and this interdependence needs to come from a commitment to get the product out into the market as quickly and effectively as possible. Groups and teams are formed as needed to make sure the product is a good fit in the market and is accepted by it. Pioneers need to be very open to product and market information, regardless of where it comes from, but that information is always focused on whether the product or service can find a way to fit into needs that exist in the market.

The culture of a Pioneer organization should be comprised of groups and individuals that come together and go their own ways, depending on the issues they are dealing with. A leader may spend most of his or her time on the outside, getting the needed support to bring the product to market. Informality and loose organizational environments work the best.

Innovation seems to thrive in the looseness or practices in the organization. This is often referred to as *slack*. Huge inventions have occurred by chance and only became known because there was enough time and interest in all that happens in the process. Silicon Valley start-ups are notorious for creating loose, informal, but highly interactive environments, in which the work of getting the product into the market is done, that operate easily together and are able to rearrange themselves as the market changes. This should occur at all levels of the organization. Any walls between functions or groups should be seen as unnecessary barriers that keep information from circulating and being acted upon.

Interestingly, it is not usually necessary to create a formal organizational structure specifically for nurturing concerted, common effort. This seems to arise naturally when the focus is on new ideas and innovative products or services.

In companies that have a long history of inventiveness and innovation, a kind of traditional environment arises that is fostered over and over as leaders come in, do their work, and eventually phase out. But the culture is maintained despite the ups and downs of the marketplace.

Examples of new young innovative companies are Google, Facebook, and hundreds of start-ups around the world, especially in pockets where they are mutually supportive, such as Silicon Valley in California.

Examples of traditionally innovative companies with a strong Frontier new product development organization are pharmaceuticals like Merck, health-care product companies like Medtronic and Johnson & Johnson, and manufacturing companies like 3M.

Organizational Archetype Characteristics

WARRIORS	HUNTERS
• Focus on lower cost/ increase demand • Driven by both internal and external ideas • Minimal outside market information needed • Market-oriented internal structure • Culture of dependence • Strong management	• Focus on meeting customer expectations & slow down margin erosion • Driven by both external & internal ideas • Outside market information is essential • Market-oriented internal structure • Culture of interdependence • Team management
RULERS	**PIONEERS**
• Focus on fulfilling demand • Driven by internal ideas • Minimal outside market information needed • Function-oriented internal structure • Culture of independence • Strong management	• Focus on developing new products • Driven by internal ideas • Outside market information is necessary • Function-oriented internal structure • Culture of interdependence • Loose management

CHAPTER FOUR

Organizational Systems and Behavior

One of the most interesting characteristics of organizations is the presence of systems that enhance the kind of work done. Systems are orderly patterns that can be seen in the way things are designed to happen or happen as a result of trying to perform tasks. Today's companies tend to be very aware of these systems and are attempting, through various IT programs, to enhance their productivity and effectiveness.

Systems then are formed around the kind of work done by the parts of a company. They are also highly reflective of the organizational competitive type in which they are working. These patterns can be detected in the way work is performed, where the attention is directed, what influences decisions most often, and how the structure of the effort is put together so that it does its assigned job adequately.

The Systems at Work in Markets and Organizations

The systems that are most important to this discussion come as a result of efforts by companies to resolve the tensions that are played out as people attempt to get the work done and be successful in the marketplace. These tensions are present in all organizations, and every company finds a way to resolve them. They come from a primary struggle in the market to create products and services that meet needs of people and, in turn, generate resources to be used broadly.

In the market, the struggle is between the kinds of conditions that allow for consistently significant resources coming from the business proposition and the ability to predict and control the marketplace so that the work can be successful. That is how the original matrix was formed, and it is how we are able to find a position that has been achieved in that struggle that represents how well the company is competing.

The visualization of this struggle allows for a diagnosis that, at the very least, tells us in what market we are engaged with our business. It also tells us about the kinds of struggles we are having getting sufficient resources (which we call margins) and how well we are doing finding a position with sufficient control in which to do the business.

So these are the primary tensions. Secondary tensions can be shown by connecting the corners of the diagram. Lower left positions in the market, for example, indicate domination. Upper right positions indicate just the opposite—that is, how much we have to share that marketplace.

Thus the market grid, and now the organization grid, becomes a kind of map to understand the dynamics that are a result of competition. Therefore, it is critical to understand these dynamics as well as have a strategy that relates to holding or improving the position. This is how we will use both the market matrix and the organization matrix in the rest of this book.

Market Dimensions Profile

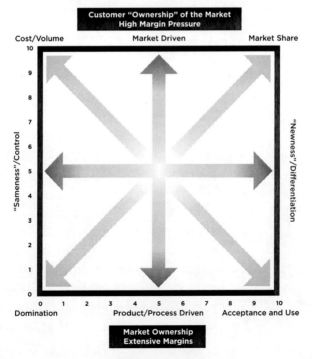

Organization Dimensions Profile

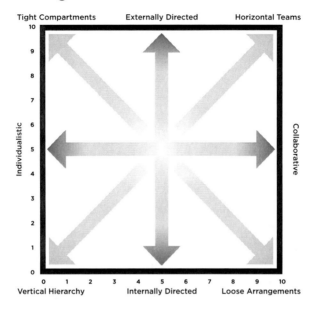

The organizational patterns in each competitive archetype are largely influenced by two factors: its natural and appropriate organizational structure and the nature of professional work relationships among its leaders and employees.

A structure is created to provide an orderly and predictable pattern of work so that others can engage in the work with ease and a clear notion of what to expect. Structures determine who reports to whom and what parts of the work are assigned to which groups of people. These structures have a lot of variability. They can be designed to enhance command and control as well as form teams that are self-directed, for example.

Our point in this discussion is that these structures and relationships form differently in differing competitive environments.

For example, in the following diagram, you can see that generally, environments that are able to be controlled and where significant demand for the efforts of the work is an expectation, vertical systems tend to proliferate. These systems take less time and energy directly (although they may spawn other kinds of political behavior) and are more appropriate in situations where domination is the preferred relationship in the market.

Vertical systems—that is, systems that foster the role of manager as decision maker and director of activity—tend to also foster domination kinds of leadership. This is appropriate for that kind of setting, although it will be clear from later discussions that this needs to be modified considerably to be sustainable. The reasonable arrangement, which you will see is located in the Ruler environment, will be to the upper left of that quadrant, which means it is somewhat modified by team behaviors that are more consistent with the Jungle or Hunter environments.

Horizontal systems—that is, systems that foster pushing decisions out toward the customer interface—that attempt to adjust activities on the run, with customers, are often characterized as teams, though this term is largely misunderstood and overused. The intention, however, is to make the organization more customer or market driven as opposed to the Ruler environment, which tends to be driven by the intention to drive products into the market rather than react flexibly to customer needs and demands.

The following diagram demonstrates visually what needs to happen in these two environments:

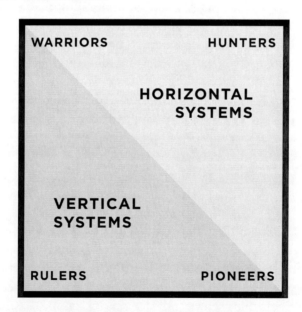

In organizations with vertical systems—mostly Rulers plus some Warriors and Pioneers—the emphasis in the organization is on efficiency and meeting high demand. These systems tend to focus on the organization itself—on deliveries, deadlines, profits, etc.—rather than on customer requirements. Such organizations perform best when they have clear delivery channels and products that are familiar and known and dominate the market. Their vertical structures serve to keep order and direct employee efforts toward internally developed goals of production and profit.

This does not imply that they are dictatorial. It simply implies that these organizational forms fit the kind of activity that is most desirable in their marketplace. At the same time, within certain aspects of the organization, teams and collectivity are present and honored. One example of this is in the new product development arena. Teams are often the vehicle used to finalize the product or service and make it ready for the market.

In contrast, those organizations that use horizontal systems—primarily Hunters—are naturally driven to create order and effectiveness for the benefit of the customer. Managers who represent groups of customers normally have more authority than function managers. Effectiveness in these systems is measured in terms of customer satisfaction as well as competitive acumen (e.g., reduction of costs). Groupings of divisions are done by the market to be penetrated and served rather than the kind of product or function that is used to create them.

Because Jungle markets are so competitive, Hunter organizations normally need horizontal structures that are close to the customer. Planning here is a function of the particular situation. The organization often needs to be able to satisfy the customer without going up and down a hierarchy for approval. The issues here are speed, preserving scarce resources, and exerting the least possible effort in order to achieve very difficult goals.

It is important to note here that horizontal systems can be quite expensive, with a tendency to slow the process down. Therefore we see companies trying to enhance productivity through process analysis to at least get unnecessary steps out of the process, especially human activities that are unnecessary to the outcome and often create issues along the delivery process.

While some companies clearly fall into one area of the above grid, others (usually Warriors and Pioneers, which both fall into cusp quadrants) may require a mix of structures. Most Warrior organizations, for example, work best if they have a combination of vertical structures that govern the whole system and smaller horizontal structures that deal with the parts, such as franchises. Both, however, are managed with tight central plans. People who work inside these systems expect that these clear, carefully delineated plans will exist and will provide them with most of their direction. Managers in the corporate headquarters of these organizations—companies such as Burger King and Office Depot—spend a good deal of their time developing these central plans. Yet those who carry out those plans on the front line are much less vertical in their management.

At the same time, recognize that the behaviors cited above represent what is happening at the very outside corners of the archetype. A position in the corners of the diagram is representing all nonsustainable systems. These must be modified considerably to be closer to the center position, which is where successful businesses reside.

Pioneer organizations also typically function using a combination of vertical and horizontal structures. They allow products and markets to evolve, and they expect less order and more freedom and redundancy. Scientists and engineers in the lab also expect this of management. As a result, these companies may employ a vertical management that is responsible for allocating resources and creating environments that support innovation. Yet within the development groups themselves, there is normally some form of horizontal management. Typically, this consists of egalitarian teams, with team leaders who support the activities of both the team and each of its members.

The type of professional behavior needed to support organizational activity and fulfill a company's central mission also varies from one archetype to another. If an organization's central mission is to manufacture and deliver a commodity product (e.g., computer disks or frozen orange juice) quickly and at a low cost, then order and control are essential. Relationships in such an organization are (and should be) based on compliance and tight adherence to central plans. Such a structure and set of behaviors enable beer companies to move millions of bottles around the world quickly and efficiently.

This does not mean there is no room for individuality in these organizations but that the balance is clearly on the side of central plans and standard, repeatable behaviors over large territories.

In contrast, Frontier markets demand innovation and discovery. These tend not to happen in centrally planned organizations. Thus the behaviors most needed in Pioneer organizations (and in some Rulers and Hunters) are a lack of standard procedure and a willingness to seek and exploit opportunity.

Culture and Values

Each archetype requires a particular type of culture that supports the organization and enables it to thrive (or at least survive and compete) in its market. This culture is made up of four fundamental aspects:

- The general *organizational climate* (and the professional relationships that characterize it)
- The organization's *structure* (and the key attributes of that structure)
- The primary *focus of leadership* (and the tools used to exercise that leadership)
- The organization's *core values*

The chart below presents the essential aspects of climate, structure, and leadership for each archetype.

	CLIMATE	STRUCTURE	LEADERSHIP FOCUS
RULERS	Compliance	Control	Power
WARRIORS	Agressiveness	Strength	Orders
HUNTERS	Achievement	Flexibility	Strategy
PIONEERS	Developement	Adaptation	Resources

Rulers need compliance—and a bureaucracy to ensure it—so that strategy can be deployed easily from the top. The organization should consist of layers of managers whose primary interest is directing the people below them, as specified by strategy. Leaders should use their power to motivate managers and employees to support that strategy. All these attributes support the market-dominating behavior expected in (and needed by) a Ruler company.

Such behavior, and the bureaucratic structures that support it, has gotten a great deal of bad press in recent years. *Yet these are precisely what enable a Ruler organization to survive, thrive, and dominate its market.* While such an arrangement may not result in high worker satisfaction, most of the people employed by a Ruler organization expect to have to deal with these attributes and learn to work with them as best they can. Indeed, people who can tolerate dominant and sometimes erratic managerial control may actually feel quite satisfied working in this kind of company.

Warriors need to act in a unified manner across large spans of geography. It is expected that a Warrior organization will act very aggressively to capture each available point of distribution or shelf space. To achieve this goal, its structure needs to be designed for strength of direction, with little or no deviation, so that huge strategies are precisely implemented through the proper execution of orders. People who are personally aggressive thus tend to be happiest in Warrior organizations.

Hunter organizations exist in a survival-of-the-fittest environment, where each accomplishment is an important contribution to the continued life of the company. Leaders must capture the minds of managers and employees by allowing them to help create—and fully understand—the strategy so that it guides behavior without aggressive managerial control. People who are relationship-oriented and who like making decisions and taking direct action tend to be successful in this environment.

Pioneers have a voracious appetite to develop products, services, and markets. The structure of a Pioneer organization needs to be very flexible in order to allow for rapid change and movement. Leaders need to concentrate on developing the resources needed to support development. These resources typically include people, money, equipment, access to raw materials, and information. People who enjoy newness, innovation, personal challenge, and intense environments tend to do well here.

Each Archetype Needs Its Own Type of Leader

Traditionally, people who write and talk about leadership have attempted to identify a set of qualities that typify effective leaders. By now, I hope it has become clear that no one style of leadership can possibly be effective in all four organizational archetypes. Each archetype needs—in fact, demands—its own particular style of leadership.

Dozens of writers have, quite correctly, pointed out the dangers of trying to run a creative, loose-knit organization using a heavily bureaucratic and hierarchical management style. *Yet it is just as much a mistake to try to run a Kingdom organization using a Pioneer style of leadership or, for that matter, a Hunter or Warrior leadership style.*

The leadership attributes needed to run, say, a Warrior organization such as General Electric are considerably different from those needed in a Pioneer organization such as Pfizer, which expends much of its resources developing and marketing new prescription drugs. For years, Jack Welch led GE like a general, with great success; this same strategy, however, would have proven disastrous at Pfizer—and just as disastrous in a Hunter organization such as Sharper Image or a Kingdom such as Microsoft. Had Bill Gates been so out of touch as to choose Welch as his right-hand man (and had Welch been foolish enough to accept the job), chaos would have quickly ensued and Welch would have quickly gained a reputation as a contentious and ineffectual manager.

In short, leadership in any organization needs to reflect the strategic direction of the company. The following chart illustrates these differences among the four archetypes.

	PERFORMANCE	DIRECTION	GROWTH
RULERS	Maximum Profit	Dominate the Market	Add Resources
WARRIORS	Maximize Effiency Reduce Costs	Differentiate Products and Cut Costs	Create Image, and Maximize Brand Value
HUNTERS	Dominate Niche	Secure Market Share	Add Value to Products
PIONEERS	Innovate and New Products	Develop Opportunity	Introduce New Products

Leadership Focus

A Ruler organization needs leaders who will drive the company to maintain or increase profit margins and grow the company's ability to deliver more and more.

Warrior organizations need leaders who are exceptionally good at continually increasing efficiency, lowering costs, and finding new ways to differentiate their products from others.

A Hunter organization needs leaders who can help the company quickly adjust products and marketing to market changes while continually adding value to its products.

Pioneer organizations need leaders who can drive innovation and new product development while maximizing the technology available to it.

The Structure of Leadership

There is yet another crucial aspect to matching leadership styles, organizational archetypes, and market environments: *each archetype has its own ideal type of leadership structure.* A breakdown of these structures looks like this.

	STRUCTURE	ALLIGNMENT	CONTRIBUTION	STYLE
RULERS	Manager-led	Management	Individual Job Performance	One on One
WARRIORS	Coordinated	Financial Concerns	Part of a Force	Cross-functional Support
HUNTERS	Flexible	Customers	Member of a Posse	Teams Everywhere
PIONEERS	Network	Technology	Risk and Innovation	Teams

Ruler organizations need leaders who are comfortable focusing on the bottom line and the delivery of products. One-on-one management tends to be the style, with heavy use of individual-oriented performance management to ensure adequate sales and delivery of products.

Warrior organizations need aggressive, financially driven, marketing-oriented leaders who will cut across functions to coordinate activity and drive down costs and who will stop at nothing to acquire new points of distribution.

Hunter organizations need highly flexible, mission-driven leaders who are able to manage teams and groups of all kinds and who are able to thrive in a very cost-conscious, constantly changing environment.

Pioneer organizations need visionary, technically competent leaders who can develop and maintain high financial and technical support for products. They need to be comfortable taking risks and must be able to put their faith in products, ideas, and people that may sometimes seem far removed from present-day reality.

Redefining Leadership

Too many of us in management have ascribed moral values to our own leaders, leadership styles, and organizations. Those who instill collaborative thinking in their employees may consider themselves better than those who manage on a one-to-one basis. Warrior leaders who are successful in doing more with less shake their heads at R&D-focused Pioneer leaders, who may spend large sums of money developing three products then bring only one of the three to market.

It is essential to understand that there is no moral issue involved here. Rather, the issue is one of organizational fit. As leaders, our job is not to practice some set of imagined managerial virtues (and avoid the ostensible leadership sins) but to create the best fit between the market, our organizational archetype, and what we and our coworkers do each day.

PART THREE

A Guide to the Four Markets

The next two chapters are intended to help you understand your company, or anyone's company, in its dynamic environment. The whole point of *Sync & Swim* is to help you determine the nature of the marketplace where a company or nonprofit does business and especially how adequately the company is positioned. To be able to engage in the market adequately, it is important to know what the context is— that is, the competitive environment in which transactions take place with products or services and whether and how the organization is constructed to participate.

Chapter 5 is a synopsis of the characteristics of the four markets and the four organizational types, with descriptions that you can use in discussing the results of an assessment of the market position and the organizational response. It provides some names and descriptors we can use to talk about our situation, especially after reading and participating in chapter 6.

Chapter 6 presents a sample assessment to get a beginning understanding of how you can find your company's position in the market and a picture of the organization's response to that position. Although the assessment is far from adequate in this form, it will provide a template to understand how these concepts can be used in real life.

In my work with organizations, the assessments of the market position and the organization's response serve as the beginning of a process to develop a strategic plan for the business. After a thorough examination of the results on these matrices, there is a wealth of information to use in determining the next strategic steps for the company.

To get an adequate understanding of the market and the organization, all the members of management take the assessment in order to formulate the way the company sees the market and the organization. It is also likely that there are clear differences between the way each manager experiences it. Working through these differences is the beginning of strategy.

CHAPTER FIVE

Organization Ecosystems

This section provides a series of one-page snapshots of the four different market environments and the organization archetypes that are best suited to each. My intent is to bring the key concepts and distinctions of the previous ideas into sharp, clear focus.

Each snapshot provides the following for one of the four essential market ecosystems:

- A brief description of the market
- The central characteristics of that market
- The organization requirements for success in that market
- What tends to create a successful business strategy in this market
- The key elements of an organization culture that thrives in this market
- The primary dynamics of the market
- The most appropriate structure for an organization competing in that market

This serves two purposes: first, it distills and codifies what has come before, and second, it provides an easy reference to return to as you make your way through this book and, hopefully, assess your company or one that you are working with or are looking at with an intention to join forces with.

Let me stress once again that none of these snapshots is meant to be an absolute or complete description of any organization. Real life rarely conforms precisely to our models of it. Consider these snapshots as useful and highly accurate templates, not perfect likenesses.

In a similar vein, none of the terms on the next four pages is meant to be taken either negatively or positively. Rather, each is intended as a partial description of either a particular market or the type of organization best positioned to succeed in it.

Rulers in Kingdom Markets

These organizations or companies are designed to

1. deliver widely desired products or services to customers,
2. generate ample profit, and
3. maintain dominance over their markets through innovation, acquisition of their competitors, and aggressive pricing practices.

Market Characteristics

acceptable high margins

high demand

predictability and stability

clear and obvious

Organization Requirements

focus on fulfilling demand

driven by internal ideas

minimal outside market information

strong management

Business Strategy

profit

react and dominate

build resources

Basis of Organization Culture

domination of market

strength

power

Market Dynamics

dominate

predictable, slow transitions

Organization Structure

orderly and controlled

vertical

function-oriented

both restricted and independent behavior

Market Assessment

BATTLEGROUND	JUNGLE
KINGDOM	
	FRONTIER

Organization Assessment

WARRIORS	HUNTERS
RULERS	
	PIONEERS

Warriors in Battleground Markets

These organizations are designed to deliver commoditized products or services to very large numbers of customers while earning very limited profit margins. Warriors compete with a small number of well-known companies offering similar products or services.

Market Characteristics	**Organization Requirements**
restricted margins	reduce cost and increase demand
few serious competitors	driven by external ideas
predictability and stability	minimal (but focused) outside market information
clear and obvious	strong, directive management

Business Strategy	**Basis of Organization Culture**
increase efficiency	aggressiveness
reduce cost	control
build resources	following orders

Market Dynamics	**Organization Structure**
dominated	orderly and controlled
predictable, slow transitions	strongly vertical and flat
	market-oriented
	both restricted and independent behavior

Market Assessment

BATTLEGROUND | JUNGLE | KINGDOM | FRONTIER

Organization Assessment

WARRIORS | HUNTERS | RULERS | PIONEERS

Hunters in Jungle Markets

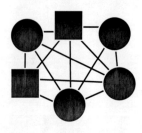

These organizations are designed to compete for a niche against many competitors whose products are highly sought after. The market has not consolidated, though it may do so in the future.

Market Characteristics

restricted margins

many serious competitors

great turbulence

complex and ambiguous

Organization Requirements

reduce cost and meet customer expectation

driven by both external and internal ideas

strong need for market information

team management

Business Strategy

dominate the niche

secure market share

add value

Basis of Organization Culture

achievement

interdependence

niche strategy

Market Dynamics

contested

turbulent and swift transitions

Organization Structure

innovative and somewhat free

horizontal

market-oriented

both independent and restricted behavior

Market Assessment

BATTLEGROUND	JUNGLE
KINGDOM	FRONTIER

Organization Assessment

WARRIORS	HUNTERS
RULERS	PIONEERS

Pioneers in Frontier Markets

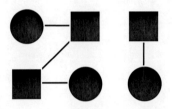

These organizations are designed to introduce new, significantly different products into existing markets or to create an entirely new market around those products.

Market Characteristics

acceptable margins
high demand
turbulence
complex and ambiguous

Organization Requirements

develop new products
driven by internal ideas
outside market information needed
loose management

Business Strategy

innovate
develop new opportunities
and products

Basis of Organization Culture

development
adaptation
interdependence
resources

Market Dynamics

open
developing markets
both horizontal and vertical

Organization Structure

innovative and free
independent behavior
function-oriented internal structure

Market Assessment

BATTLEGROUND	JUNGLE
KINGDOM	FRONTIER

Organization Assessment

WARRIORS	HUNTERS
RULERS	PIONEERS

CHAPTER SIX

The Archetype Assessment

This chapter introduces the Archetype Assessment, a widely used (and highly practical) instrument for determining which market archetype your own organization is best suited for and which one it is doing business in right now.

I have used the Archetype Assessment successfully with organizations of all types and sizes in several countries for the past twenty years. Over time, I have refined and updated it to make it as valuable and accurate as possible. (The full assessment is available at www.JackTesmerInstitute.com).

In this chapter, you will use a sample of the Archetype Assessment to evaluate your own organization and its current position in the marketplace. Your organization's score will begin to tell you about what it is doing well, what it is doing poorly, and what it needs to do differently in the future.

The assessment can also be used very effectively with other organizations—e.g., to analyze your competition or to look more closely at a firm that seeks to acquire or merge with your own.

Initially, however, let's look at how you can use the assessment as a tool for determining

- what market your organization currently competes in,
- what market it is best suited to compete in,
- how close a match exists between your organization's culture and its chosen market, and
- how your organization may need to change in order to be more successful or to simply survive.

Like any evaluative instrument, the Archetype Assessment should not be used alone. When combined with your own experience, the experience of others, and some common sense, however, it can have great value as a means to better understand your organization and its market; as a tool for creating understanding, agreement, and buy-in; and as a way to initiate serious strategic discussion.

To get a better understanding of how we get positions in the market and the organizational response, we are suggesting you answer two questions for each of the four major market and organizational dynamics to see what your issues might be and to get an idea of how this assessment is used in an organizational setting.

To get an idea of how the full assessment works, think of an organization that you would like to assess for whatever reason. Then answer the next eight questions to the best of your knowledge by evaluating on the 0–10 scale the response that best fits your situation.

Market and Organization Assessment
(Sample Version)

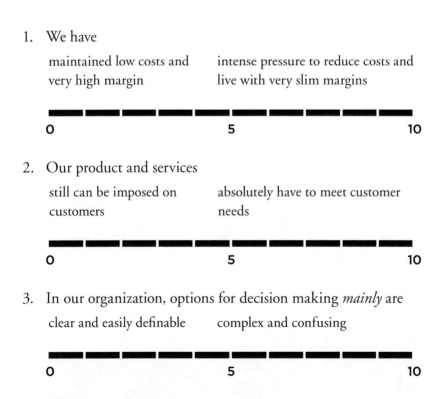

1. We have

   | maintained low costs and very high margin | intense pressure to reduce costs and live with very slim margins |

   0   5   10

2. Our product and services

   still can be imposed on customers   absolutely have to meet customer needs

   0   5   10

3. In our organization, options for decision making *mainly* are

   clear and easily definable   complex and confusing

   0   5   10

4. To meet the expectations of our marketplace, we need

    simple and efficient technology   complex high technology

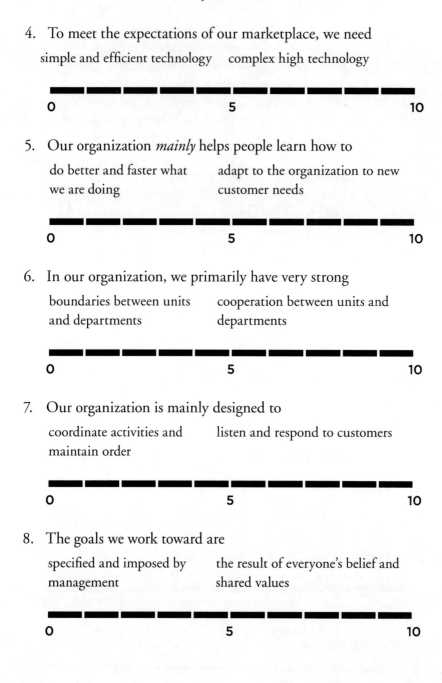

0   5   10

5. Our organization *mainly* helps people learn how to

    do better and faster what   adapt to the organization to new
    we are doing   customer needs

0   5   10

6. In our organization, we primarily have very strong

    boundaries between units   cooperation between units and
    and departments   departments

0   5   10

7. Our organization is mainly designed to

    coordinate activities and   listen and respond to customers
    maintain order

0   5   10

8. The goals we work toward are

    specified and imposed by   the result of everyone's belief and
    management   shared values

0   5   10

Calculation of Scores

Market Score
Add 1 and 2 and divide by 2 =_____ (place on graph on vertical axis)
Add 3 and 4 and divide by 2 =_____ (place on graph on horizontal axis)
Create the coordinate on the graph; this represents the market position.

Organizational Score
Add 5 and 6 and divide by 2 = _____ (place on graph on vertical axis)
Add 7 and 8 and divide by 2 = _____ (place on graph on horizontal axis)
Create the coordinate on the graph; this represents the organization position.

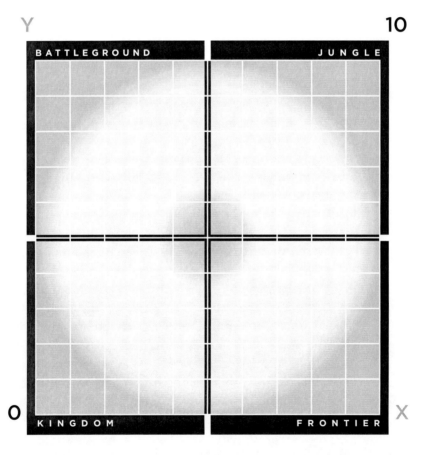

A Key to the Descriptors

The questions in the Archetype Assessment are designed around four *market descriptors* and four *organizational descriptors*, which you will recognize from previous chapters. The four *market descriptors* are the following:

- The availability of *resources* (e.g., people, capital, and raw materials)
- The degree of *competition*
- The complexity of relevant *technology and market characteristics* (e.g., how hard it is to meet customer needs and/or use the relevant distribution channels)
- The stability and predictability of *business opportunities* (e.g., the likely extent of future competition and/or the economic, political, and regulatory climate)

The four *organizational descriptors* are the following:

- Your organization's *receptivity to new information* about itself, its markets, the relevance of its mission, and how well it is functioning.
- *Interdependence*—how well your organization manages collaboration, especially internally, but also with other organizations that are necessary for delivering its products and/or services to customers.
- *Market orientation*—whether your organization builds its structure and culture primarily around serving customers or primarily around accommodating its own internal functions.
- *Strategic focus*—whether in making strategic decisions, your organization relies primarily on external information (customer satisfaction feedback, changes and innovations by competitors, national and regional economic changes, etc.) or on internal information (sales goals, process problems, inventory levels, etc.).

Keep in mind that the purpose of this assessment here is to demonstrate the process and will only give you an idea of what the full assessment process is like.

The full forty-question assessment will create a much more accurate picture of your own business and organization as it actually functions, not an idealized vision of what it could be or a replication of the sugarcoated image your communications people may publicly disseminate. The more honest you are in your answers, the more accurate and valuable the assessment will be.

Your Most Important Choice

Perhaps you've already said to yourself, "Wait a minute! What does this author mean by 'my organization'? Is he talking about the division I work for? the specific department in which I work? the company as a whole? the multinational Fortune 500 firm that owns the company? Each of these operates quite differently. Which one can I legitimately call 'my organization'?"

This is a critical question—but it's not hard to answer. As you complete the Archetype Assessment, you should consider your organization to be the entity

- whose performance, competitiveness, or bottom line you want to improve;
- to which you want to make a greater contribution; and
- where you are able to make a genuine difference.

A general knows his troops and their capabilities and creates a battle plan that makes the best use of those capabilities. However, until he is aware of the conditions under which his troops will be fighting, he will not be able to organize them for success on the field. Becoming aware of these conditions for your own organization is the purpose of this assessment.

Remember that the Archetype Assessment is a highly practical tool, not an academic or theoretical exercise. Its purpose is not to get key people to say, "Gee, isn't that interesting?" Rather, the assessment has been designed to help managers understand the conditions of battle and to either change those conditions or change their battle plans to best respond to those conditions.

The full assessment has forty questions to give it adequate depth and breadth. At any point, you can go online and make use of the digitized version that will not only show your positions for both the market and the organization but will also provide an in-depth interpretation that will be useful to you and others who are participating with you. To do so, follow these instructions:

1. Go to www.JackTesmerInstitute.com
2. Follow the instructions to take the assessment.
3. When you are finished, a report will be sent to your e-mail address. The report will contain a visual representation of your position in the market and your position in the organization. For each of these, it will describe the conditions that one would expect with a score such as you received, the issues to be resolved, and the kind of change needed.

This is just the tip of the iceberg, so to speak, as there is a wealth of information to be gathered first in each of the results of the market and the organization and in comparing the scores to each other. This book will provide some of that information, but only with time and use will you be able to see the full spectrum of information that is available.

It is also a very revealing exercise to engage your fellow team members in comparing their scores. We have experienced in most management teams a significant difference in their scores, indicating that they are really playing out of a different playbook from each other.

A Quick Comparison

The next chapter will help you make the most of your assessment results. However, you can immediately make two very important judgments just by glancing at your grid now.

First, you can see which market archetype your organization is currently best suited for and which, for all practical purposes, it currently acts as if it is operating in. (In many cases, this is also the market environment it *should* be operating in.)

Second, you can quickly tell how close a match there is between your organization and its chosen market. The closer together your star and circle are, the better a match there is between your organization and the market it competes in.

If you look closely at your grid, you'll see that it is broken up in two ways: into four large squares, each representing a different market archetype, as well as into sixteen smaller ones.

If your circle and star are in the same market archetype *and* in the same smaller square apart, congratulations! Your organization is already well positioned to succeed, and it will probably need to make only minor adjustments in order to maximize its success.

If your circle and star are farther or in different market archetypes entirely, then your organization probably will have some serious work do to. The farther apart the two are, the more wide-ranging the required changes are likely to be.

All this is just the beginning, however. Your organization-market profile can tell you a great deal more. So roll up your sleeves and turn to the next chapter, where you'll start digging deeper.

CHAPTER SEVEN

Interpreting Your Own Assessment

In this chapter, you'll begin to turn the concepts in this book into large and tangible benefits—both for you and your organization—by interpreting the results of your organization-market profile in detail. You'll do this by doing the following:

- Identifying the competitive nature of the market in which your organization *currently competes*. (This is indicated on your grid with a star, which is the result of your answers to questions about your organization's resources, competition, technology, and business opportunities.)
- Examining how your organization *is currently designed to function* in relation to the four market archetypes. (This is indicated on your grid with a circle, which is the result of your answers to questions about your organization's receptivity to new information, interdependence, orientation to its market, and strategic focus.)
- Measuring the gap between how your organization operates and the market in which it *currently competes*.
- Determining the kind—and the magnitude—of change that your organization *will need to undergo* in order to succeed if it decides to continue to operate in the current market.

All this will be done by looking closely at the grid, which is broken up in two different ways:

- The four quadrants represent the four basic market archetypes.
- Each quadrant is broken up into 100 mini quadrants, each with its own unique characteristics.

Identifying the Nature of Your Market

Market environments vary according to

* intensity of competition,
* amount of turbulence, and
* degrees of complexity.

Place a mark indicating the scores for the market and a mark for the organization on the following grid

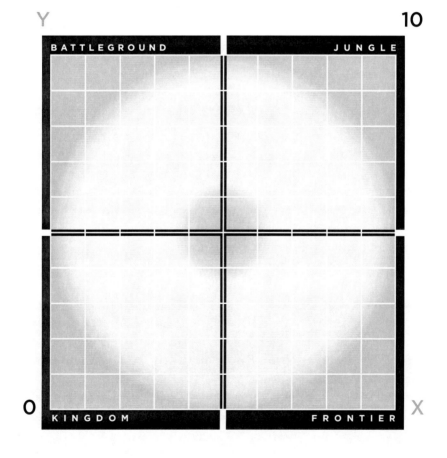

Use the following reminders to interpret your scores.

Kingdom markets are characterized by abundant resources that come from adequate margins and/or budgets, simple (or at least internally understandable) products and technologies, and stable or predictable conditions. Normally, a single successful company dominates such a market.

Battleground markets are resource scarce (i.e., they have very tight margins and budgets) and highly competitive. Products and services are well understood and usually commoditized. Each such market typically contains a small number of competitors, most or all of which are well-known. There is an intense concentration on reducing cost and waste while increasing quality and efficiency. Margins are very slim, and organizations survive by dealing in extremely large volumes. The key issue is usually moving as much product as possible to as many points of distribution as possible, as quickly and inexpensively as possible.

Jungle markets combine the conditions of scarcity with complexity and turbulence. Products and services are difficult to produce and distribute, yet buyers demand that companies both inexorably reduce costs and produce steadily better and more consistent products or services. Market conditions change rapidly and are influenced by multiple, uncontrollable outside forces—e.g., governments that know little about production processes. Jungle markets are often transition states between Frontiers and Battlegrounds.

Frontier markets focus on innovation and development. Either margins are high, providing sufficient resources to support the development of proprietary new products and/or customized services, or investment money is readily available to continue the development process. Products and services are new and not widely understood. Many of the market forces are difficult to predict, making life on the Frontier risky and opportunistic.

Each of these four market archetypes is subject to a range of variation, which means that it's possible to get considerably more detailed about the market your organization now competes in. The following chart contains some of that detail:

MARKET

	BATTLEGROUND		JUNGLE	
	Very low margins Very restricted resources Highly identified, deadly competition Highly predictable market Very clear and obvious market structure	Very low margins Very restricted resources Highly identified, Deadly competition Predictable market Clear and obvious market structure	Very low margins Very restricted resources Highly identified, deadly competition Turbulent market Complex and ambiguous business environment	Very low margins Very restricted resources Highly identified, deadly competition Very turbulent market Very complex and ambiguous business environment
	Low margins Restricted resources Serious, identified competition Highly predictable market Very clear and obvious market structure	Low margins Restricted resources Serious, identified competition Predictable market Clear and obvious market structure	Low margins Restricted resources Serious, threatening competition Turbulent market Complex and ambiguous business environment	Low margins Restricted resources Serious, threatening competition Very turbulent market Very complex and ambiguous business environment
	Acceptable margins Sufficient resources Demand for products Highly predictable market Very clear and obvious market structure	Acceptable margins Sufficient resources Demand for products Predictable market Clear and obvious market structure	Acceptable margins Sufficient resources Demand for products Turbulence with many opportunities Complex and ambiguous business environment	Acceptable margins Sufficient resources Demand for products Great turbulence with many opportunities Very complex and ambiguous business environment
	Very large margins Unrestricted resources Strong demand for products Highly predictable market Very clear and obvious market structure	Very large margins Unrestricted resources Strong demand for products Predicable market Clear and obvious market structure	Very large margins Unrestricted resources Strong demand for products Turbulence with many opportunities Complex and ambiguous business environment	Very large margins Unrestricted resources Strong demand for products Great turbulence with many opportunities Very complex and ambiguous business environment
	KINGDOM		FRONTIER	

You will find it instructive to review and compare the descriptions in all the different mini quadrants, particularly (1) other mini quadrants within your market and (2) the mini quadrants adjacent to yours. As you do this, you may notice that *the four mini quadrants closest to the grid's center offer the greatest opportunities for success.* In general, these mini quadrants are good places for markets (and organizations) to be. Indeed, the best of all possible worlds is for your organization and its market to be plotted side by side, close to the center of the grid.

Examining Your Organization's Design

Now let's look more closely at your organization and its structure. Begin by noting the quadrant and the mini quadrant in which your circle is plotted.

Organizations vary according to the following:

- Whether they respond primarily to the needs of their customers (i.e., they are market driven) or the needs of the organization (i.e., they are function driven).
- Their extraversion or introversion—that is, the direction of their communication antennae. Are they focused on what's happening in the market because that market is so demanding and difficult, or are they focused on what's going on inside the organization because there is time to internally reflect and because the market is relatively safe and stable?
- The amount and range of outside information they value and use and the way in which that information penetrates the organization. Does it flow quickly through an interdependent system, or does it percolate slowly through a hierarchy with clearly defined boundaries?

The following figure shows how your grid reflects these key aspects of your organization:

- The speed with which the organization reacts and adapts to outside information.

ORGANIZATIONS

BATTLEGROUND

- Extremely aggressive market attitude
- Very high cost consciousness
- Strong productivity orientation
- Great focus on internal control/cost
- Highly directive management/Generals

- Extremely aggressive market attitude
- Very high cost consciousness
- Productivity orientation
- Focus on internal control/cost
- Directive management/leaders

- Aggressive market attitude
- Fighting for market share
- Great focus on internal control
- Highly directive management/generals very concerned with costs

- Aggressive market attitude
- Fighting for market share
- Focus on internal control
- Directive management concerned with innovation and costs

JUNGLE

- Extremely aggressive market attitude
- Extremely customer needs oriented
- Resource conscious
- Participative management
- Cross-functional business/process teams concerned with adding value

- Extremely aggressive market attitude
- Extremely customer needs oriented
- Extremely resource conscious
- Highly participative management
- Business teams, networks, alliances very concerned with adding value

- Market responsive
- Customer needs oriented
- Resource conscious
- Participative management
- Cross-functional business/process teams concerned with adding value

- Market responsive
- Customer needs oriented
- Extremely resource conscious
- Highly participative management
- Business teams, alliances, network, very concerned with adding value

KINGDOM

- Internal operations and function driven
- Production oriented
- Great focus on internal control
- Very deep hierarchy/rules/bureaucracy very concerned with profit

- Internal operations and function driven
- Production oriented
- Focus on internal control
- Hierarchy/rules/bureaucracy concerned with profit

- Very internally and function driven
- Completely production oriented
- Great focus on internal control/profit
- Very deep hierarchy/rules/bureaucracy very concerned with profit

- Very internally and function driven
- Completely production oriented
- Focus on internal control
- Hierarchy/rules/bureaucracy concerned with profit

FRONTIER

- Key function driven
- Concern for product acceptance
- Market reactive culture
- Loose and friendly management

- Key function driven
- Concern for product acceptance
- Very market reactive culture
- Very loose and friendly management

- Very internally and key function driven
- Deep concern for product acceptance
- Market reactive culture
- Loose and friendly management

- Very internally and key function driven
- Deep concern for product acceptance
- Very market reactive culture
- Very loose and friendly management

Ruler organizations are closed, independent, and isolated. They are organized around functions and driven primarily by internal considerations. They flourish in abundant, simple, stable markets, which they are able to dominate. They enjoy high demand for their products and/or services and consistently attempt to move toward stability.

Warrior organizations operate with the internally driven, hierarchical style of a clan. This enables them to survive in low-margin, resource-scarce, and highly competitive markets. As such a market becomes increasingly competitive, Warriors become somewhat more flexible, but they still remain internally focused and able to quickly influence large volumes of product or services. Warriors are both highly aggressive and highly defensive. Their goal is to maximize the use and accessibility of their products and services.

Hunters are flexibly structured organizations that are highly interdependent with their markets. They have developed systems that allow them to track and respond to rapid and highly unpredictable market changes. Their key attribute is versatility, and their focus is on innovating and marketing products into niches of need.

Pioneers are flexible, loosely organized organizations that can respond quickly to changing conditions. Although they function in unpredictable markets, they can succeed by earning good or excellent margins on new products. Their focus is on moving new technology or innovations into the market. Their key characteristic is opportunism.

Measuring the Gap

An important part of the results on the grid is the distance between the market score and the organizational score. The further the distance, the more significant the problems will be for driving any strategy. The amount of difference in these scores will give you some idea about the change effort that will be demanded.

Analyzing Your Score

If distance between the market score and the organizational score is small (one or two blocks or numbers, unless there is a double line between them), then your organization is already ideally positioned to succeed in its market and probably does not need to make any significant changes. If the difference is several blocks and includes a double line, it's probable that nothing short of a top-to-bottom transformation will do.

If the distance is one to two blocks, a near fit exists between your organization and its market. While nothing of substance needs to be done soon, continuous improvement is important for keeping your organization efficient, competitive, and strategically focused. These changes will probably seem significant to many people within your organization. However, improvement projects should be a continuous part of everyday organizational life.

If the distance is three to five blocks, the gap between what your organization does and what it needs to do is significant. Some serious cultural issues will need to be addressed in making the necessary changes. It could require deep, sweeping cultural changes.

In this grouping, if management wishes to continue in its current market, it needs what I call a *culture break*. Its basic assumptions, values, beliefs, and behaviors—i.e., the basic building blocks of its culture—all need to change substantially. If they don't, the organization simply won't be able to succeed in that market.

This means your organization must redefine its sources of both energy and synergy. Very significant change needs to occur in how

- tasks are completed,
- the organization is structured,
- rewards are given out,
- information is made available,
- technical systems are used, and
- decisions are made.

If your organization is more separated than that, it has a very serious problem on its hands because its culture is very much out of sync with its market. Management needs to *immediately* begin completely rethinking and redesigning the entire organization. This process typically has three stages:

First, make a few immediate and drastic changes to stop the red ink from flowing and begin generating some reasonable margins. This usually means (1) changing the way cash is moved in and out of the organization, (2) getting rid of any significant and obvious unnecessary costs, and (3) reducing the number of employees where it will make the greatest difference.

Second, you will need to completely retool the organization and redesign the way it does business. Many of its top executives will need to go, and much of management will need to be changed as well. There must be an infusion of new people from outside the organization and/ or from those parts of the larger organization that are performing well (and that score well on the organization/market profile). This new management needs to create a very practical strategic plan and short- and long-term accountabilities.

Third, you will need to build a new, more appropriate structure and culture from scratch.

Each of these activities is a major change process in itself and will require strong leadership, enormous commitment, and a willingness to face the considerable (but necessary) pain of transformation.

David Nadler has created a very useful grid that explains what generally occurs in each of these three processes. I have adapted it slightly for use here. This can be a guide to the kind and extent of the changes that should be contemplated as a result of the assessment process.

TYPES OF CHANGE

	IMPROVEMENT	CULTURE BREAK	TURN-AROUND
Driving Force	Internal efficiency	Anticipation or awareness of Market shift	A survival threatening market shift
Focus of the Change	Individuals, processes, Specific departments and/or units	People, core competencies, and systems: performance, direction, and growth	The whole organization, and most, or all, of its people
Speed of the Change	Usually rapid	Slow, with growing commitment and ownership	Rapid at first, then slow and steady
Role of Senior Management	Provides general support	Drive the changes; install persistence and a sense of urgency	Drive the entire change effort; make tough, big decisions
Types of Change	Relatively minor—department and unit changes not affecting the total system	Major changes—focusing on structure, alignment, roles, management style, operating systems	Organizational transformation which affects everyone. Changes the nature of the business, and ultimately restores equilibrium
What Happens to Key Players	Nothing	Some may be replaced	Many or most are replaced

Adapted from David Nadler

This can be a guide to the kind and extent of the changes that should be contemplated as a result of the assessment process

By now, you have probably realized that evaluating the alignment between your organization and its chosen market is not a one-time practice. *It should be a continuous effort to make sure that your organization is in the most advantageous position to compete and win in its chosen market.* Since the nature of any market is dynamic, and since some markets can change overnight, it is important to evaluate your organization and its market continually.

The actual adaptation or transformation of any organization does not happen by accident, by a CEO issuing an edict, or by management trying to institute whatever culture is described in the latest issue of a management journal. *It happens by understanding the competitive nature of your market through continuous research and dialogue and by understanding the organizational archetype that best serves that market.*

The hard (and crucial) part is actually creating the right culture and continuously adapting it as the market changes. The following chapters will assist you in that process.

CHAPTER EIGHT

Practicing Sync & Swim

The exciting part of coaching sports activities comes when there is data about the other team to use in planning an approach to the next game with them. It is this data that forces the examination of how the team will match up with the opponent and the development of a strategy to use in the coming encounter.

The results of taking the PerfectBizMatch Assessment perform a similar function for management as it develops its strategy in the marketplace. The results of the assessment create a picture that can be dissected in multiple ways that provide options to take into account in a successful strategy.

At the very least, the assessment, with the results arranged on a graph, will signal the major issues in the market and in the organization that will be significant factors in setting and implementing strategic initiatives.

Our purpose in this chapter is to practice interpreting some sample graphs in order to develop some proficiency in using the new data and to show its power to inform managers about the sync-and-swim issues in their organization.

Example #1

The Market Assessment

The first example, and these are all actual cases (with the names and some of the conditions changed to protect the business), is a commercial painting company with a gross income of about $25 million. It is family owned and has been in business for some twenty years.

The following grid will show the results of both the market and the organization. It gives the results of four members of the management team. The squares each represent the position that is served in the market by the company in the eyes of the four management team members. The circles represent the view of the same group of the nature of the organization that is presently in place to serve that market.

Market/Organization Position

Commercial Painters
$25 M Gross Receipts

■ MARKET
● ORGANIZATION

BATTLEGROUND / JUNGLE / KINGDOM / FRONTIER

Market Position

Here are some questions you can begin to answer by observing the grid:

1. In general, what is the major market archetype that is served?
2. Assuming that they are actually in that market, what is the quality of their functioning in that market? Are they earning a

satisfactory return on their product or service? Are they taking risks and finding opportunities that do create some tension but also provide differentiation and innovation?

3. Finally, is the management team in sufficient agreement about that market that allows them to develop a strategy that has common acceptance and support for its implementation?

Our Interpretation

Considering that they do commercial painting, which is characterized by a bidding process where the lower price wins the job, it would seem that they are seeing their market as a commodity or Battleground. There are not many competitors, and they tend to each have a major market share. It also appears like they have sufficient control and differentiation in the market to be able to engage in the enterprise with sufficient profit to continue the business. They have control of their business and production processes at least to their satisfaction. One person has some concerns about margins that could be significant (that person may be the financial officer!).

In terms of a potential strategy for the future, it would seem that they are poised to continue to grow in a significant manner and should be looking at potential acquisitions and/or mergers.

The Organization Assessment

We now look at the assessment results of the same company but focus on how the organization functions. The following questions could be asked:

1. Which quadrant are they positioned in as far as an organization is concerned?
2. What is their relative position in that quadrant in terms of viability? Are they near the center of the grid? If not, where are they and what are the major issues that they are facing?
3. Do the majority of the respondents end up in the matching quadrant on the organizational grid (e.g., in this case, they

should be in the Warrior quadrant)? This is an important question from the point of view of the general culture that seems to be accepted by management.

4. Are there large discrepancies between the individual scores, and what could be the reason for that?

5. How would you describe the situation to a consultant you hired to help improve and grow the business or a venture capitalist interested in purchasing the business?

6. What assumptions could you make about their ability to implement an aggressive growth strategy or implement a new set of infrastructure systems?

Our Interpretation

Either their organization needs to become something different to serve the Battleground market or they need to rethink their market position and offering. They are obviously in the wrong quadrant for a Battleground or commodity market.

They have the organizational profile of a company whose market should be in the Jungle—that is, a highly competitive market with many players attempting to keep margins that can support that kind of activity, needing great flexibility and collaboration. Thus they are probably attempting to work collaboratively and are probably forced to because of a lack of organizing systems that make cooperation easy. Chances are, in the parlance of the industry, they are probably organized as a "job shop," where each contract is done differently.

This is also a very expensive operation for a Battleground market. Working together is expensive by nature. This is not unusual in a family-owned business. There is nothing inherently wrong with this kind of organizational culture. However, if the market is really in the Battleground, that is, a commodity market, the margins cannot support that kind of organizing. Volume, speed, and low cost are the ruling dimensions or should be!

Changing this kind of culture is extremely difficult and is often not accomplished until the business has been sold outside of the family.

The Combined PerfectBizMatch Assessment Results

When viewed together, the significance of the difference between the position in the market and the organization is seen visually and is quite impressive. In this case, there is no match between the two scores. That would indicate that the belief is widely held that what is present in the organization is perceived as the only way to do it even though that might not be true at all. We see this kind of dichotomy in family-owned businesses that are still run by the first generation or in a company with a very strong founder who treasures the camaraderie involved in starting and developing the early stages of a company.

In this company, which on the surface is doing well, it will be difficult to take any other route to growth than to attempt to grow it little by little, experimenting along the way for a means to keep the organizational model and, at the same time, grow. If the new growth is in the Jungle market, there could be some synergy available as it will be quite easy for people to get the work done in that kind of market—there is a natural fit.

But there then is a consternating factor; how does the new business fit with the old business? This can be a major struggle internally. If there is an attempt to change the culture so that growth can happen in accordance with the market opportunity, the change will need to be deep and complete as there is a significant difference in mentality and systems between these two models.

Although this is an actual case, it is quite unusual for the scores to be that concentrated in both grids. I am using it as a means of demonstrating the power of prediction available in using the grid. If I were acquiring this business, I would need to have a significantly powerful strategy in mind as it would be a major shift in culture or business and many of the players would probably not survive, especially leadership.

The most important question of all is as follows:

> What business and organizational issues will I face either in attempting to market our product or service or implementing a new system or changing leadership or purchasing another company, improving the climate in the company, or adding a new product line or any one of the many improvements and innovations that are tried often by today's managers?

The assessment results present the backdrop in which these initiatives are made and will surely affect the result. All strategic actions need to be preceded by this kind of analysis, at least!

Example #2

The following grid represents the results of the assessment taken by a family business marketing and maintaining recreational vehicles. They sold the whole range of vehicles from pop-up trailers to high-end luxury liners. The business had been willed to the five children of the original owners and had continued the business for a few years, when they decided to create a strategic plan that all six children and their families could use to develop the business together in the next years.

The strategic planning began with all five taking the assessment and determining what the present situation was. The following diagram indicates the various positions that were held by the members of the family.

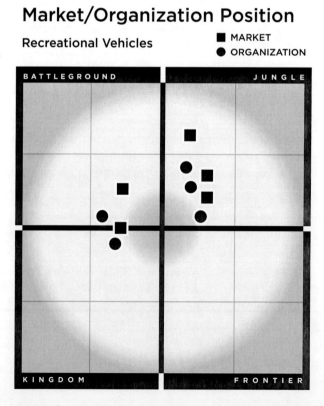

Market/Organization Position

Recreational Vehicles
■ MARKET
● ORGANIZATION

There were considerable discrepancies among the five as demonstrated by the graph.

Three people saw the business as a competitor in an open market with lots of competition, two are feeling that the margins were rather acceptable, and one was very concerned about the margins generated by sales. Two others saw the business as a commodity where consolidation had already taken its toll and a few players were left, with the margins very reasonable for that market. They saw the market as consisting of a few large players with different brands that essentially shared the market among themselves. They believed that it was really all about price competition, with service being there only to stay abreast of the competition.

At the same time, the organizational scores followed in a similar pattern. The three in the Jungle experienced the company in a kind of Hunter format, highly collaborative, willing to do anything to keep a customer. The other two saw the company in a Battleground with a kind of Warrior mentality: get the order, move the trailer off the lot, get the customer out the door, and wait for them to come back for service. Going beyond that was not necessary. Little collaboration was needed since they had many control systems in place.

It was finally determined, after several group sessions, that the best quality of the business was the fact that the family worked well together, that the business was highly competitive and resided in the Jungle, and that innovation and service were highly effective and that the real quality of the organization was its family atmosphere and togetherness. A new business plan was developed, the youngest brother was chosen as the CEO, each of the siblings took a major role in the company, and they have been very active competitively in their region.

Example #3

The final grid comes from a magazine publisher that services a specialty group that is part of the infrastructure of most large organizations. It supplies ideas, research, examples, etc., that are useful to members of these groups. At one time, these services were part of large companies but, in the 1980s, were mainly outsourced. The business model was to provide the magazine and its content free and to secure revenue from advertising. As the twenty-first century rolled in, with data available everywhere, the company questioned their future even though sales and margins were holding steady.

In this case, we will show the grid results and then provide a number of questions that need to be answered to get a good idea of the position of the company in their market and the kind of organization that supported that business. You can draw your own conclusions about what their condition actually is and what steps they needed to take strategically.

The company was run by the second generation, represented by four brothers who had learned the business from their father.

The grid is as follows, and the kinds of questions that need to be asked also follow. This is a chance to see if you can generate some better questions and some answers to the ones listed so that you would have a good sense of what should happen in this company as they try to grow.

Market/Organization Position

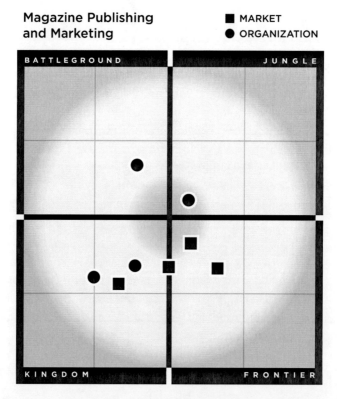

Market

- What actual market seems to best represent the focus of the company?
- How much agreement is there on that actual position?
- What seem to be the issues they have concerning sustainability?
- What seem to be the issues they have concerning sustainability in the market?

Organization

- What kind of organization best describes what is prevalent in this company?
- How much agreement do they have at the top of the company concerning the type of organization they experience?
- How congruent is the organization with the market they seem to serve?
- What are some of the organizational issues you can predict are or will be occurring?
- How serious are the issues in the market and those in the organization?
- What kinds of changes would you recommend to this company?
- Market position?
- Kinds of margins being acquired?
- Key strategic business issues?
- Management understanding?
- Necessary strategic changes?
- Does the organization match the market?
- What changes are needed to match the market served?
- Are there individual issues that will need to be solved?
- What is the seriousness of these issues, and what kinds of change are recommended?

The interpretation of the grids that result from the assessment is first done automatically by the software that supports it. Each person will get an interpretation of their scores and a description of some of the conditions they can look for.

However, the real power of the process is to have all the key decision makers take the assessment and together compare scores and derive potential learnings from the multiple positions on the grid. This lifts people's gaze to the kind of abstract level needed to work on strategy, the beginning of which should be an understanding of the environment in which business is done and the way the organization is structured to help it attain its goals.

PART FOUR

Transforming Your Organization

CHAPTER NINE

Becoming a Hunter Organization

In a Jungle market, companies compete relentlessly to attract and retain customers by attending to their every desire. This is typically combined with an equally relentless drive to reduce costs in the supply chain. As a result, Hunter organizations need to

- eliminate traditional hierarchical thinking,
- place the decision-making power as close to the customer as possible,
- get products to move through the supply chain as quickly as possible, and
- create highly committed, highly flexible organizational groupings.

In this chapter, we'll look at how organizations move into a Jungle environment and what needs to take place within those organizations in order for them to become successful Hunters.

There are five ways in which your company may enter (or find itself in) this market:

1. *Getting pulled in*—you offer a product or product line that is experiencing significant competition for the first time.
2. *Slipping in*—you are part of an industry whose products and/or services are no longer new and where competition is becoming more intense.
3. *Diving in*—you are a start-up company or business unit entering a contested environment.
4. *Being pushed in*—your product or product line is moving from a dominant position to a highly contested one.
5. *Forcing a way back in*—you're attempting to move out of a commoditized Battleground environment by changing

the nature of your products, your methods or channels of distribution, or both.

Here's what these five variations look like on the market grid:

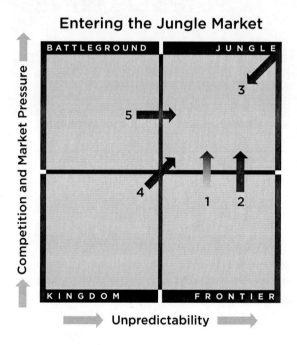

Entering the Jungle Market

Let's take a closer look at each of these five situations and how you and your company can best deal with them.

1. **Getting pulled in**

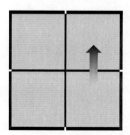

Your company offers a product or product line that is experiencing significant competition for the first time.

After a time, new products introduced by Pioneer organizations almost invariably experience competitive pressure. At this point, you have a choice: learn to succeed in a Jungle environment (and make the necessary changes); sell or discontinue the product and refocus your attention on other, newer products; or redesign the product so that it is essentially new once more.

Key Issues

If your organization decides to continue with the product and to compete in a Jungle environment while also offering products new to the world in a Frontier, your most pressing concern is how to live in both markets at once with their differing business and organizational needs.

You will have to split the company into two separate entities so that it can maintain or grow its market share in a Jungle market without losing the open, entrepreneurial atmosphere necessary for innovation (a strict necessity for success in the Frontier). These two business units must operate quite differently: the Pioneer organization will continue to be very individual oriented and driven by functions such as research and development or marketing; the Hunter unit will be customer oriented, market driven, and highly collaborative.

Your top-level management will need to begin to balance its need to allocate resources for innovation with the pressures of cost and customer needs. At the top, your managers will begin to feel caught between growing and/or maintaining a customer base and developing new products. There is no magic wand that will solve this dilemma; your executives will simply have to choose the balance that they feel will best serve the company.

Common Difficulties

- *Losing the innovative edge*

Customer demands for quality, and service becomes ever present. This puts great pressure on the entrepreneurial structure used to foster innovation. More and more of your time and resources get spent in developing trust and cohesion among marketing, production, and sales so that markets are served well and efficiently.

This usually means that less time and fewer resources are allocated to the laboratory. As the frenzy of the Jungle replaces the excitement of the Frontier, management can no longer exert control on technical concerns in the same ways that were acceptable and comfortable in the past. The old system is simply too cumbersome to react quickly and effectively to customer needs.

Today's Internet start-up companies will soon be in this environment as the market becomes flooded with thousands of small companies that want to make some money through e-commerce.

- *Tracking the competition*

Although the competition emerges gradually, it tends to grow at an ever faster rate. What looked like minor competition two months ago may suddenly be taking huge bites out of your market share. In other cases, some new technology may suddenly emerge to create unexpected competition. Most Pioneer organizations are not fond of spending their time searching out and studying the competition. (Usually, they are too busy convincing potential customers of the superiority of their products and services.) But at this point, watching and keeping up with the competition will have become an absolute necessity.

- *Getting market leadership*

Technology people tend not to be market or customer oriented. However, they often think that they are and that they understand the market better than anyone else. What they actually do understand, however, is not the market but how *their* customers react to *their* products.

In Pioneer organizations, these technology folks usually have managerial authority over most product-delivery functions. At this point, however, these people can easily become major obstacles to change. In the past, their answer to market challenges has been to develop new products, not to lead changes in marketing or in the organization.

- *Creating a market culture*

Involvement in a Jungle market requires a different kind of involvement and a very different organizational culture. It becomes critical to make sure that many kinds of teams are used and that people are well trained and able to work together smoothly. (Unfortunately, such efforts are often not invested in.) You will need to recruit a different breed of marketers and salespeople: those who can work well in a very customer-oriented environment.

Solutions

Starting immediately, organizational decisions need to support both Hunter and Pioneer business units, which must be separately maintained. Unless both cultures and structures are maintained in an open and conscious manner, both will suffer.

These separate operations cost money and management time, however. This is an investment issue and needs to be treated strategically as one.

It is common for companies to split off some or all the functions of business units whose products are moving into the Jungle. Typically, production and/or management gets moved to a new location. In some cases, it makes sense to create an entirely new organization with its own culture and management structure.

A Hunter organization needs to be led by people with a high sensitivity to the market, competition, customer needs, and financial concerns. These people tend to come from marketing. However, *they may be hard to find in the marketing department of the Pioneer organization since that department has not been attuned to these types of information during most of its life.* As a result, people with the necessary skills may need to be recruited from outside your organization. Unfortunately, even though they may be indispensable to your success, once they are hired, they are not usually valued by the rest of the organization.

Your top leaders will need to inspire confidence and trust in these new people as well as in the directions that the new strategy takes the company.

As for the leaders of the new Hunter unit or organization, they need to be intensely competitive by nature. They must be able to develop a strong linkage between marketing and all other functions in support of total product quality and the lowest possible cost of manufacturing and operations. (This is not at all how most Pioneer marketers work; they tend to be out in the field, finding new customers and building the customer base.)

Adaptation Issues

• *Creating the separation*

Separating out part of your organization will almost certainly not be easy. The people who have had jurisdiction over this product may need to be reassigned and replaced. This typically results in friction, turf battles, resignations, and a moderate amount of distress.

You'll need to create this separation with the future in mind. The change needs to be led by marketing but with strong support from your technology people. Rituals will be needed to help the technical people let go of product management yet not give up their support for the product.

• *Moving fast*

By the time it is necessary to take this kind of action, it is usually zero hour, if not considerably later. It is important, therefore, to speed up the decision-making process and move along the organizational design process quickly.

• *Providing strategic support from the top*

This move must be part of a general strategy for the company so that internal stakeholders do not see it as a knee-jerk response to a scare in the market.

All the changes—and more importantly, the strategic reasons for them—need to be communicated clearly and openly in advance. Straightforward, unambiguous communication (and perhaps deliberate overcommunication) needs to occur at every step so that people will accept the change and help it take place.

There is also the strong possibility that your company might get carried along with the market and end up with most or all its products inadvertently moving into the Jungle. This is what happened for Hewlett-Packard in the early 1990s. This possibility also needs to be clearly communicated to everyone in the organization so that if this situation does come about, people are at least somewhat prepared for it.

2. **Slipping in**

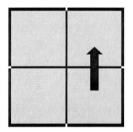

You are part of an industry that is no longer oriented primarily toward new products.

Your company's whole product line is losing its proprietary hold on the market and is now experiencing considerable competition on all fronts. You are now forced to retain or grow market share in a very turbulent environment, very likely in the midst of steadily decreasing prices.

Your products are no longer considered innovative. You must now compete on both quality and price. Continued improvements will merely enable you to stay in the game, not win it.

Key Issues

There is no turning back. Your whole industry is heading toward a Jungle environment, and your company must either redesign itself to function in that environment or get out of the business. Nothing you or your organization can do will stem the tide toward commoditization of products because this is an industry-wide movement. If you want to retain your Pioneer culture, then you will need to focus on significantly new products and sell off or discontinue the old product lines.

If you do decide that your company will compete as a Hunter, you need to determine whether it is possible to carve out a large-enough niche to create the margins needed to support continued product differentiation.

Apple struggled with this issue for nearly ten years. Finally, with Steven Jobs's return, the company found a niche that was large enough to support innovation and that kept its products from becoming commodities (at least temporarily). By focusing on style and design as well as functionality, the new Macintoshes became the best-selling personal computers in their market niche.

Common Difficulties

- ***Changing the mind-set***

The Frontier tools and strategies for survival remain part of the organizational mind-set, but they are not necessarily what is needed in the Jungle. Yet this mind-set is not easy to change, especially if (as is often the case) management is completely overwhelmed by the complexity of doing business in this new environment.

- ***Changing the focus to the customer***

Pioneer organizations tend to be vertically designed so that the technical function can have the freedom and the power to lead the system. In the Jungle, however, the problem is to drive the system horizontally based on the demands of the customer. It is difficult for the technology function to give up leadership to a new, market-driven system.

- ***Moving from individuality to collaboration***

Pioneers honor individuality while Hunters honor collaboration. A quick (and usually difficult) transition needs to be made from a culture that values individuality and innovation to one that values collaboration.

This will be a permanent change that everyone in the company must make. The change needs to be driven by top management and requires the involvement of every employee. If this change is not made, particularly at the management level, the functioning of the organization will be seriously impaired.

- ### *Learning what customers want*

A Frontier organization is designed to invent new products and take them to a market that is waiting for those products with more or less open arms. The company simply needs to focus its attention on letting everyone know that its products are there.

In contrast, a Jungle market requires companies to really understand their customers and to meet all their needs. This typically means making the products easy to purchase, own, and use. Therefore, throughout the organization, people must stop believing that they know what is best for the customer and instead begin gathering information on what its customers actually *do* want and demand.

- ### *Outgrowing the arrogance of technology*

The arrogance of technology must be overcome. In many Pioneer organizations, there is a sense that the most important parts of the business are their products and their capabilities. In a Jungle environment, this is no longer the case; customers may make buying decisions based largely or entirely on speed of delivery, price, and/or ease of purchase (everything else being more or less equal). If your company can't provide exactly what the customer wants—readily and at a reasonable price—then they may simply go elsewhere. The entire organization must therefore make a shift from revering its products to serving customers.

Solutions

If you intend to succeed in the Jungle, you must first redesign your processes, structure, management, and culture to reflect a strategic focus on your customers. This is admittedly an extremely tall order. Yet it can be done—*if* your organization commits itself to the following:

- Determining exactly who your customers are
- Discovering what they want and demand (not what you think they want or think they *should* want)
- Focusing on quality, price, and delivery
- Differentiating each of your products and product lines in at least one significant way

In addition, you will need to create a new environmental search-and-design function whose job is to (1) constantly evaluate the market and (2) quickly adapt both your products and your marketing to changes in the market—ideally, ahead of the competition. You will also need to allocate significant resources to the creation of product and brand distinctiveness so that your products are easily recognized, desired, and differentiated from those of your competitors.

Lastly, you will need to begin paying strict and constant attention to becoming more efficient while still meeting all customer needs. This requires innovation, something you're used to. But now the innovation needs to be focused at least as much on keeping costs down and quality up as on creating new and differentiated products. To do this, you'll need to create cross-functional teams to examine all your processes.

I cannot overstress the importance of this last set of tasks. If you ignore them, your margins will continually erode.

Yes, these undertakings are all daunting, but your organization's very survival depends on performing them.

Adaptation Issues

It is critical to slow the deterioration of margins as much as possible while still giving customers the best products or services. This means paying close attention to the end of the supply chain and providing lots of feedback to all parts of the chain. The big danger is letting margins shrink to the point where they suck the life out of your organization.

At the same time, you'll need to simplify your processes and information systems so that they help people focus on meeting customer expectations and so that they do not take too much of the company's resources and attention away from your customers.

Resources need to be allocated into your marketing function so that the right market niche is developed (or discovered) and exploited. Management has to step up to the plate to lead this process by creating permanent internal structures that reinforce this new customer-oriented activity.

It is critical that you select people with the right attitudes and skills to lead all these changes. You will almost certainly have to bring in some key players from other Hunter organizations.

3. Diving in

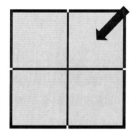

You are a start-up company or business unit entering a contested environment.

It is quite possible to succeed and even thrive by entering an already-contested marketplace—but only if your products or services are a natural fit with your existing capabilities (and thus, you have low product development costs). To try to enter a Jungle without such a fit is usually folly because you simply won't be able to obtain the margins you need.

The other way to successfully dive into a Jungle market is to serve your customers so well that you can charge slightly higher-than-average prices and thus create the margins you'll need to cover market entry costs. This may enable you to triumph over companies entering the market with Pioneer cultures and histories of serving Frontier markets.

Key Issues

First, you must be able to offer products that have a proven demand. You cannot afford either the time or the expense of any significant market testing. Your organization must also be able to mobilize resources quickly in response to sudden (or changing) opportunities that may present themselves.

If you are already an established name seeking to enter a Jungle market with a new product line, your reputation in other markets can be a critical factor in opening distribution channels.

Common Difficulties

- *Addressing both efficiency and customer service*

It is essential to determine the niches that you can exploit with great care. Otherwise, the normal and inevitable evaporation of margins can occur too quickly. That means that you need to stay very carefully attuned to your customers' needs and just as attuned to producing your products very efficiently and effectively.

- *Avoiding complacency*

There is absolutely no room for complacency—or even for temporary stasis—in a Jungle market. Sometimes, the only difference between success and failure is a willingness to seek out markets that have been underexploited. It also behooves your company to be open to adding products or services that have already proven successful even if they may not fit with your company's earlier image. You may have to choose between sticking with your tried-and-true product lines and going under or staying competitive by adding an unusual new product line.

- *Becoming externally competitive yet internally collaborative*

One much less obvious—yet potentially insidious—difficulty is the nature of competitiveness itself. Because a strong competitive drive is essential for success in a Jungle market, that competitive drive may manifest itself internally, with employees trying to outdo and undermine each other. This can create enormous internal friction that is, to say the least, highly unproductive. Much time and energy may be wasted on internal battles, and as a result, the company may not mobilize quickly enough to adequately respond to opportunities or customer demands.

- ***Getting commitment to products***

It can sometimes be difficult to get your people strongly committed to "me too" products since there is no long-term development phase. They may (quite correctly) see the company as feeding off the work of others and perhaps (less correctly) of undercutting the hard work of Pioneers.

- ***Avoiding burnout***

The Jungle is intensely competitive. There are strong pricing pressures from other brands, particularly from the companies that led the way out of the Frontier into the Jungle. This intensity can drain people emotionally unless bureaucracy—particularly its negative aspects—is held to a bare minimum. Burnout is very common because people are managing very large markets and producing larger and larger volumes with fewer and fewer people, usually relying increasingly on technology to hold it all together.

- ***Getting up to speed***

In a Jungle market, it is usually very difficult to get up to speed with the competition in meeting customer expectations for quality and predictability. Starting up a new Hunter organization is a bit like boarding a train going one hundred miles an hour.

- ***Finding leaders***

It is absolutely critical to find the right people to lead your foray into the Jungle. Simply finding the correct people can be a very difficult task, yet you *must* find them and get them on board because you know how dire the results of operating with the wrong people will be.

Solutions

Your organization is most likely to succeed if you focus your resources on the customers at the end of the supply chain. This means working backward from the customer to solve any problems. This can best be done through cross-functional teams that are built around trust and communication. Such teams are able to create collaborative work environments that focus people's attention outward rather than inward. As a result, these teams may be the means by which your company maintains the margins it needs to support the internal work.

You will also need to redesign your organization's structure so that there are as few levels of management as possible. Ideally, people should be organized according to customer niches. Use teams wherever possible to solve the very difficult problems brought on by combining low cost and high quality.

Adaptation Issues

Introducing a new product requires a huge commitment of resources, yet in a Jungle market, products need to be introduced quite quickly and efficiently. If you specialize in entering markets already occupied by new products, then you will have already developed a culture and infrastructure that will support your entry.

If the culture and infrastructure for doing this are not yet in place, then they need to be created. This is an enormous task because your company has not yet learned the lessons about a Frontier market that tell you what priorities are critical to success.

Your success will also be related to the kinds of alliances you have in this market. This is a big part of life in the Jungle. You need to be able to reach out to other producers (or other parts of your supply chain) to get resources that your organization simply cannot provide. You will more than likely never be able to maintain all the essential links in that supply chain on your own.

Whatever new market you are entering, there are experienced people throughout the industry who know that market niche extremely well. You absolutely must find them and bring them into your organization, either as leaders or consultants. They will be invaluable in helping to guide strategy and to keep the company from allocating very scarce resources based on a gut decision alone. (Industry experience and detailed market knowledge are crucial leadership attributes in the Jungle.)

You must also be able to clearly differentiate each product or product line in some way in order to support it in its niche. Such clear differentiation becomes crucial in the Jungle, where customers can normally choose from among a large field of competing products. Even though you may be selling "me too" products or services, they must have more than merely "me too" value to your customers.

You need to be able to put together a team that can invade this market with a "me too" product. This often means coaxing talented people away from your competitors. These folks can land on their feet and start running as soon as they arrive. Acquiring them, however, takes considerable resources and lots of flexibility in negotiations. (And don't expect them to stay to help build long-term capacity in your organization.)

Entrance into a Jungle market is also a somewhat temporary endeavor. The competition at some point will begin to consolidate, and eventually, the market will develop more and more attributes of a Battleground.

4. **Being pushed in**

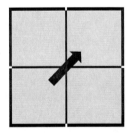

You are moving from a dominant position to a highly contested one with a particular product or product line.

After years of operating in a Kingdom market, enjoying proprietary status over a product or product line, you may find yourself suddenly (or not so suddenly) challenged by one or more competitors. This often is the result of some new technological innovation or the expiration of a patent or copyright.

The intense struggle that followed may have pushed some of your product lines into the Jungle. This creates a demand for new ways to produce these products and a need for new structures to support those processes. During the past decade, this has happened to many of the companies that were Rulers in the '70s and '80s.

Key Issues

Companies that are forced into a Jungle market are seldom happy with their predicaments. The strategic intent of Rulers is to keep products so well protected that they are never subjected to the kind of competition that goes on in the Jungle, yet virtually, every product or service eventually winds up in either a Jungle or Battleground market.

So if you have been pushed from a Kingdom market into a Jungle, you are probably a reluctant (if not kicking and screaming) player. In all likelihood, your company is designed to protect its interests, not to launch an attack on the market.

You will need to change this orientation and fast. If most of your company's products are sold in a Kingdom market, then operating in the Jungle will be intensely foreign to your culture.

The central change your organization needs to make is to learn to fight for a share of the market rather than to protect your lock on much or all of it. This requires new behaviors in production and operations. It also means expending significant resources on studying and selecting your customers so that you can concentrate on certain markets where you have a chance to dominate.

Like it or not, your company will need to do some major downsizing to reduce costs. You will also need to redesign your internal systems to respond to external demands much more quickly and effectively.

Common Difficulties

• *Increasing the speed of decisions*

Traditionally, Rulers are not speedy competitors. They tend to move slowly because management is many levels apart from its customers.

Unless you move your decision-making processes closer to the action, your company will be in trouble. This means that you will have to eliminate some or all the checking processes that management has used in the past to maintain control.

- ### *Redirecting attention*

Rulers are more attuned to their internal needs and to production and delivery issues than to customer demands. In a Jungle market, however, this focus is a recipe for failure. You will now need people who are finely attuned to the market. Internally derived numbers are no longer very useful; your people will now be looking at different numbers and for different reasons. Accountability must change from delivering product to holding and satisfying customers in all ways.

- ### *Showing people to the door*

Most Ruler managers have a difficult time letting go of control, and for some, it's outright impossible. Those for whom it is impossible must be reassigned to a different unit (one that operates in a Kingdom market) or else given notice.

- ### *Changing individuality to collaboration*

Ruler cultures foster and reward individual accountability. As a natural result, Rulers tend to build functional silos that are useful under Kingdom conditions. These barriers are anathema to meeting customer needs, however.

Your managers must understand the need to collaborate across the system and must be trained to do so. If they cannot, they may seriously hobble the company.

Even when people are willing to make the change, getting this large-scale teamwork to happen and supporting your teams with the supply chain information they need can be very difficult.

Removing the boundaries between silos is a major task that many people will resist. The only way to make it work is if, from the beginning of the change effort, power is allocated differently at the top of the company.

- *Getting product across the functions to the customer*

The toughest challenge of operating in your new market environment is finding ways to force products and services across the system to the customer as quickly and efficiently as possible. This means you must focus on processes rather than simply on delivery.

Yet most Rulers are stuck in delivery mode, in which products move from one function to the other, pushed by some product manager. This process will no longer do the trick. It will need to be replaced with a process centered on customer satisfaction.

- *Changing the decision-making process*

The knee-jerk reaction of many Ruler managers is to bring important issues to some kind of committee. This ensures that no part of the system is aggravated by a proposed strategy. However, these committees will now work directly against your success in a Jungle market. The whole process takes a great deal of energy and resources, which are now needed elsewhere, as well as lots of time, which the company can no longer afford to spare. This is an extremely common issue, one that makes moving from a Kingdom to a Jungle market exceptionally difficult.

- *Stifling the Hunters*

In Ruler organizations, management's role is to supervise and control. Indeed, that is what it does best. Unfortunately, when conditions begin to change and competitors have much more of a say in the market, management does what it knows best and attempts to exercise more surveillance and control. This has the effect of stifling Hunter activity. Management direction then becomes perceived as meddling. This becomes a source of considerable contention and resentment, especially by those employees who work with or close to customers.

- *Practicing frugality*

Rulers have become comfortable with the presence of ample financial resources. Ruler managers thus tend to approve most sensible requests for financial support. People generally get most of what they want, and they get used to getting it. This generosity can spell disaster in a Jungle market, where frugality is not merely a virtue but a necessity.

Managers now need to solve problems creatively and inexpensively rather than just by spending money. Ruler managers are not skilled at this.

The management control boundaries used in Ruler organizations surround functions such as manufacturing, sales, marketing, and technology. These boundaries are very useful in organizations that can focus on delivery in a demand market. However, they are anything but useful in a Jungle environment. They slow things down, take a lot of energy, and are very costly.

Solutions

Any solution must begin with some significant form of new leadership. Somewhere, a person in a key, highly visible position must lead your organization forward by example. This person usually must be new to the organization and must have a reputation for demanding or inspiring Hunter behavior. They must also be (or become) a symbol or icon for Hunter attitudes and actions in everyone's eyes. Furthermore, what they do in their first few months should firmly reinforce this reputation.

This new leader needs to present a vision of how things need to work, and they need to support that vision with a redesign of the key processes that affect both quality and cost. When these designs go into effect, the leader needs to provide substantial rewards for all successes achieved as a result. They also, of course, need to *not* reward any of the old ways of doing things.

Finally, it is important that, from the beginning, this new leader be empowered to find (and if need be, hire) the people who are able to support the change. They can then use these change agents as the nucleus of the new system, building around them. This sends early clear messages to everyone in the organization about what the new rules and culture will be.

Until and unless this kind of strategy is followed, it is next to impossible to make the needed changes, even though there may be many attempts by people throughout the system. (These attempts are helpful nevertheless because they are early warnings of what the company will need to do and be like. Unfortunately, the people behind these attempted changes tend not to last very long.)

Adaptation Issues

Ruler managers bring together all the individual pieces of a system by exercising power, but both power and politics often go awry in a Ruler organization when the market changes because what was known and taken for granted is no longer true. Therefore, it is important that power be used to begin the transformation process since employees expect power to be wielded and are used to seeing it employed.

However, this use of power needs to be focused on reducing or eliminating the siloing, segmentation, and multilevel structure so that people can collaborate more easily.

Everyone in the system needs to develop skills for working together collaboratively. This is perhaps the most significant issue for Rulers who are forced to become Hunters. These skills simply will not be developed unless they are very clearly modeled by the people at the top of the organization and unless those people communicate exactly what they want and expect from employees. This refers not only to internal teamwork and the kind of management that enhances it but also to understanding the market and customer needs. Everyone in the system also needs to know how to continually redesign processes to survive in the ever-changing Jungle environment.

5. **Forcing a way back in**

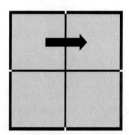

You're attempting to move out of a commoditized Battleground environment by changing the nature of your products, your methods or channels of distribution, or both.

Essentially, this involves climbing out of the fire back into the frying pan. Your organization is trying to force its way out of a Battleground, where high volume and low margins define the market, into a Jungle, where there are more players, more innovation, greater competition, and generally better margins and where success is not so heavily reliant on volume.

An almost perfect example is Snap-on Tools. Back in the early 1990s, Snap-on saw that its very good margins were steadily eroding. Top managers realized that the market was changing from a Kingdom to a Battleground and that, more and more, the company would be competing with Sears and a few other firms on volume and low margins. Snap-on made a decision to move back into the Jungle with a new product line. The company purchased several diagnostics and under-the-car tune-up companies—a natural fit since Snap-on already had ideal access to mechanics through its dealership program. Over time, as the hard tools business gets more commoditized, these new companies will account for more and more of Snap-on's business.

Key Issues

The major change your company needs to make is to become thoroughly customer oriented. In many ways, this change is similar to the one Rulers must make when they are pushed into the Jungle. However, your company is better off because its leaders and employees already understand how important efficiency is to the organization's success.

However, this focus on efficiency and lowering costs can be a double-edged sword. You must not allow this drive for efficiency get in the way of reacting swiftly and well to customer needs. Your focus must be, first and foremost, on giving your customers what they demand.

In a Jungle, you may face many competitors, and some of them may enter the market from unexpected directions. For example, Hewlett-Packard or Mitsubishi might suddenly begin competing with Snap-on in the computerized diagnostic market. Indeed, this would be as natural a move for them as it was for Snap-on because of their production capability in computer technology.

You'll also need to make a significant change in the way you market your products. In a Battleground market, your focus was on constantly increasing visibility and the number of points of distribution—in other words, pushing as much product through the system to as many locations as possible. In a Jungle market, however, your marketing energy is better spent (1) identifying customers in the niche area you select, (2) reaching out to them, and (3) satisfying them.

Common Difficulties

• *Understanding the magnitude of the change*

The biggest potential problem is not realizing how big a change your organization will need to make. A structural change is insufficient. Unless you are going to add or spin off a separate unit to address this new market, your old organizational culture will need to undergo a thorough transformation.

This will probably be resisted, perhaps vigorously. Because you've been operating on a Battleground, your people probably function with an aggressive, almost military mentality. This can become a serious deterrent to the kind of innovation needed to serve customers in a Jungle market. You will have to convince your employees—particularly your marketing people—not to support the product at all costs and go after sheer volume but to take a more interactive role with customers. They will need to start listening to what customers want and be willing to give it to them. They will also have to let go of a great deal of their control and let the people closer to the customer make more of the decisions.

Ultimately, you will need to get everyone in your organization to shift their attention to creating customers and serving them with their whole beings. This is a major change from creating distribution points and stocking them well so that advertising campaigns can be successful.

• *Getting access to customers*

It is also essential to focus on gaining better access to customers. In a Jungle, access is typically controlled by the prevailing distribution system. The market is often viewed as a zero-sum game by wholesalers and retailers, who believe the customer has only so many dollars to spend, regardless of the number and type of products offered. As a result, they tend to resist new products.

- *Learning niche marketing*

Your people out in the field will also have to deal differently with customers. Salespeople in Warrior organizations are used to implementing huge, carefully planned marketing strategies. You must now get them to understand the niche your company is moving in to. They also need to learn to secure and satisfy customers, not by making plenty of product readily available but by discovering and satisfying their needs. Suddenly, your salespeople have to do very hands-on, customer-driven work rather than just establish new distribution points. This mentality change is very difficult to make, and you should expect significant turnover in your sales and marketing departments as your organization works through the process.

- *Saying good-bye to the hero manager*

Warrior companies tend to create hero managers, especially at and near the top. They get the big ideas, and others implement them. In a Jungle, this mentality will be counterproductive and very frustrating because the ideas needed to satisfy the customer cannot be created at corporate headquarters. They must be created in collaboration with the customer by your people in the field.

- *Waiting for management to do it*

The natural corollary to the hero manager is an organization-wide belief in management solutions to marketing and implementation issues. This belief will also get in the way of understanding and serving customers.

- *Jettisoning the functional mind-set*

The separation of company functions that works so well on a Battleground becomes a detriment when serving a Jungle market. Getting across the boundaries to meet customer needs becomes of paramount importance, yet this becomes very difficult unless some major design change is implemented to break down these boundaries.

Solutions

Because a huge cultural shift—indeed, a full-blown organizational transformation—is needed to be successful in the Jungle, top management needs to very deliberately retrain its army from a squadron of fighters to an occupation force. At every possible level of the organization, starting from the top, leaders need to talk less of the power of volume and more of customer needs, innovation, teamwork, and total quality in all functions.

Everyone who in any way deals with customers needs to be trained in a new set of marketing skills, skills based on listening to and understanding the customer. If done properly, this will lead to increased innovation and efficiency in meeting customer needs.

The system itself will also need to undergo a crucial change process. You'll need to redesign all the key processes that affect your customers. I cannot overstress the need for this structural change. Without it, Warrior behaviors will continue throughout much or all of the company, no matter how much management tries to change it.

Finally, the process of setting prices needs to change so that it reflects added value to the customer rather than what can be added at each point of distribution. This is another cultural change that will almost certainly be resisted and that can be overcome only through strong communication and action from the top.

Adaptation Issues

In order to successfully adapt to your new Jungle environment, your company will need to establish a culture of collaboration. At first, this will seem foreign to many employees and many leaders as well. As a result, a significant number of people will leave on their own, and others will need to be let go. This is natural and appropriate.

A collaborative culture cannot function if only some of the people in the organization believe in it. The task of learning to be customer focused is immense; everyone has to be on board or your company simply won't be able to compete.

You'll need to establish teams and collaboration in all company activity. In essence, you'll create what has come to be known as a boundaryless organization. The Warrior culture of commonality and responding to orders will need to be transformed into a culture of collaboration and innovation, where teams come up with solutions to seemingly impossible demands in order to create greater profits. This kind of innovation not only demands energy and brainpower—it *requires* teams. It simply cannot be performed by a few very bright individuals.

Lastly, you'll need to establish a new kind of accountability. Rather than rewarding increases in volume, the new system needs to account for the ability to gain and retain market share by meeting customer needs (which, in turn, creates higher margins).

In many ways, Jungle markets are the most difficult and complex markets to operate in. Most companies that enter a Jungle market do so not by choice but because they are pushed, pulled, or otherwise forced into it, yet those organizations that do thrive in the Jungle often create some of the finest products and services and often have the most satisfied customers.

All this makes successful Hunter organizations some of the most rewarding companies to work for or lead.

CHAPTER TEN

Becoming a Warrior Organization

A Warrior's primary concerns are (1) not allowing prices to erode so far that profit becomes impossible, (2) continually striving to maintain or increase market share, and (3) creating a strong brand whose products, though similar to those of competitors, are viewed as superior in some way.

Products in a Battleground market tend to gradually lose their ability to sustain a reasonable price. At some point, however, the few companies left in the market reach a stalemate or some kind of mutual awareness and do not allow the price to get any lower. Without this plateau effect, some (or even all) of the companies would end up having to discontinue the product. Indeed, when such a plateau is not naturally established, certain desirable commodity products cease to be offered at least for a time. (Eventually, some organization will enter or reenter the market, usually at a higher price point.)

Warrior companies must push hard to improve efficiency, which is one way to improve margins. They also tend to put great effort into gaining any advantage over their competitors that might allow them to increase volume (and if possible, the price). Marketing departments continually try to find innovative ways to create desirability for their products; hence, efforts to sell beer using characteristics such as coldness (an elusive idea at best) or soft drinks via unmeasurable attributes like refreshment.

Unlike in Kingdom markets, where significant product innovation is vital, innovation among Warrior companies typically occurs at the edges of a product—e.g., in its appearance, shape, options, small conveniences, or typical customer experience. Very small changes may drive huge marketing events. Remember the introduction of New Coke or the unveiling of Domino's differently shaped pizza box? Because products have become commodities, there is usually little room for innovation outside of (1) marketing and (2) developing new ways to reduce production costs and increase sales.

At the same time, management typically establishes favorite highly efficient patterns that control all aspects of production and sales. These become "the way things are done here." Management's role is to ensure that these patterns are followed and assiduously supported by the infrastructure. The desired result is ever-cheaper production of products in ever-increasing volume, with no sacrifice of quality.

Understandably, automation and computer technology have become central to Warrior enterprises. These reduce headcounts and greatly influence corporate culture. Indeed, many Warriors' manufacturing plants operate with only a few people on site, and their role is to make the plant ever more efficient. There is usually a lot of room for teamwork, particularly in attempting to bring down costs and improve efficiencies, but this is usually at the level of the line worker. The situation is similar to foot soldiers on the front acting in concert.

Whatever its strategy, a Warrior organization needs to be able to implement it quickly and effectively *throughout the entire system at once*. A special kind of culture is needed to do this well. Such a culture requires strong product leaders (who function not unlike generals), functional leaders, a limited hierarchy, and loyal workers who are ever willing to follow orders and strategies.

There are two ways to enter a Battleground market:

1. Survive as one of the winners from the Jungle.
2. Drift into this market from a declining Kingdom.

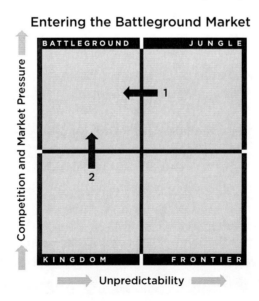

Entering the Battleground Market

Obviously, these are vastly different ways of entering this market—the first by design and very much based on success, the other by default and resulting from a significant loss in market share. Let's take a look at what needs to be done in each situation.

1. **Survive as one of the winners from the Jungle.**

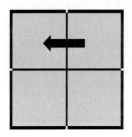

Your company merges with or acquires others in your industry, forming a larger organization with a more integrated line of products that have become commodities. You will eventually share the market with a few other large players, who are also consolidating to offer their products more efficiently.

In the Jungle, there is strong competition from many sources. No one dominates the market for any significant length of time. Eventually, however, competitive pricing creates a need for efficiency in production. Once all competitors have found all the ways of improving production efficiency that they can, there is nowhere else to go but to consolidate to achieve even more efficiency from scale or volume.

When product lines or industries reach this point, it is a natural progression to create a Battleground market through mergers and acquisitions. The banking industry, for example, has been moving in just this direction—out of the Jungle and into a Battleground—for the last decade. Banks and other financial institutions have been steadily consolidating to form huge national and multinational companies, which in turn are merging to create even larger institutions.

The credit card industry has also developed over time into a Battleground with only a handful of major players (American Express, Visa, Discover, and MasterCard) who, together, all but own the business. They battle it out through advertising and the acquisition of points of distribution, but there are few real differences between their products.

Car manufacturing and air travel are also steadily moving out of Jungles and into Battlegrounds.

Key Issues

To survive as a newly formed Warrior organization, you will have to quickly and efficiently cut through all the cultural differences of the merged pieces and form one institution with a single clear identity. Currently, each unit or division has its own culture and practices, some of which may be in conflict with those of other new partners. These differences will quickly need to be superceded by the creation of a new, strong, dominant metaculture.

From the time when the merger is first being planned, you must have a plan for working across all the different businesses and cultures. Otherwise, some very dangerous sparks will fly as they did, for example, when General Electric acquired NBC.

It will also be necessary to build (or redesign) systems that must now work across multiple organizations in order to create lower costs and/or larger volumes. Indeed, two of your major objectives should be to (1) arrive at the absolutely lowest manufacturing and distribution cost as quickly as possible and (2) move products through the organization to as many new and existing points of distribution as you can.

Your organization's new focus should be on efficiency and speed. Customer satisfaction should now be based on delivering products to buyers in the way they typically want them rather than providing great customer service and customized responses to individual needs.

In order to create adequate margins, you will need to use brand names to set prices as high as you can. At the same time, however, the cost of each product needs to be perceived by customers as minimal (or at worst, typical and reasonable) for the industry. This perception of value can be developed on a large scale through advertising and marketing (rather than at the point of customer contact, as would be done in a Jungle market).

Customer satisfaction (and the addressing of legitimate grievances) remain important; however, these should no longer be ensured by high customer contact but by constantly improving systems. The most critical customer issue for airlines, for example, is on-time departure.

Most people will tolerate lackluster service, narrow seats, and inedible food so long as they can be at their destinations on time. (This is why airlines and airline pilots are so insistent upon pushing away from the gate at precisely their departure times.) This is clearly a system issue rather than one that can be addressed through a bevy of well-trained customer service representatives.

In your new Warrior organization, decisions and plans must now be made at the top then rapidly, efficiently, and consistently carried out. At every contact point between top management and your customers, there needs to be a culture based on the carrying out of orders and a willingness to go forward without questioning or changing those orders. These orders may sometimes seem to go against common sense, but they must be followed to the letter nonetheless.

The airline industry gives us a classic (and common) example: because of bad weather, several of an airline's feeder routes into O'Hare will be delayed, yet the connecting flight to New York will leave the gate on time (and two-thirds empty), temporarily stranding dozens of connecting passengers who arrive at the gate a minute or two later.

A Warrior organization should not have many levels of authority since each level eats up time and energy, both on legitimate activities and on internal politics. This means that most managers will need to have very wide spans of control. For example, literally two hundred sales representatives may answer to a single local or regional sales manager. These supervisors will primarily need to organize and monitor activities rather than build personal relationships and facilitate cooperation. This is an enormous change from a Hunter culture, which typically operates with small teams and managers who function more like coaches.

Perhaps the biggest change of all will be that much of a person's organizational life will now be fixed and in the form of orders. Individuality should be permitted (and in certain situations encouraged) but only in how orders are carried out, not in how relationships are created with customers. Highly innovative and highly relational people will not thrive in these conditions, so it is in everyone's best interest to identify these people, encourage them to go elsewhere, and provide them with reasonable severance packages and strong references.

Common Difficulties

- *Allaying the suspicion of competitors-turned-allies*

When Hunter organizations are consolidated into a new Warrior corporation, longtime rival companies suddenly find themselves on the same team. This can be seriously disorienting for some managers and employees, especially those with highly competitive natures. At first, these people's natural inclination is to be on guard and to continue to compete with their old opponents.

In some cases, this will be played out in terms of previously competing organizations that have now become sister units or divisions. More often, however, this competition focuses on people's counterparts in one or more of these new units. This is especially common among leaders whose units or divisions will eventually be merged with other parts of the company in order to create efficiencies. Everything else aside, these people are in danger of losing their positions and will naturally compete against each other to keep them.

This can create a situation in which, despite directives from top management to consolidate and remove obvious redundancies, leaders of parallel divisions dig in their heels, resist all attempts at redesign, and expend much of their energy trying to preserve their power domains. In such a situation, any redesign concept will have to come from the top; in addition, it may be necessary to oust or reassign some (or even all) of the division leaders. This can be agonizing for everyone involved, but it must be done in order to replace redundancies with efficiencies. It can take a great deal of time and energy to get rid of the power domains and competitive cultures that were necessary for survival back in the Jungle. While these tend to be most visible at the top, they may exist at virtually any level of an organization. Sometimes, these residual power groups manage to maintain a kind of underground coalition that survives for years, working to benefit its hidden membership in terms of promotions and policy development.

- *Shifting the type of talent needed*

People in Hunter organizations have developed a variety of skills that are necessary in the Jungle. Typically, these include locating, selling to, keeping, and satisfying customers one at a time. Each Hunter organization thus develops its own collaborative customer service unit (either official or unofficial) that relies on people at transaction points to make case-by-case decisions that heighten customer satisfaction. In fact, it is fair to say that in Hunter companies, the focus of all company systems is on customer satisfaction through case-by-case modification of products and services. Small banks, for example, modify their services for each customer by being open to their special needs. When these banks merge (or are taken over), creating a huge national or international Warrior organization, this high level of customization becomes a drag on the new company.

To compete in a Battleground market, such individual customization must fall by the wayside. Instead, *systems themselves* must be redesigned so that most of the needs of most customers are fulfilled most of the time. There is a trade-off here. Customers will have to forgo some of the services that were provided by the small bank. In exchange, they will be offered lower costs, other services, and/or more access points (more branches, more ATMs, more ways to bank in person and online, etc.). Those who demand the old array of services will be forced—and expected—to go elsewhere. Once a company has jumped out of the Jungle into a Battleground, it needs to let these customers go without a backward glance.

The most difficult aspect of this change actually has to do with managers and employees, not customers. A different set of skills and talents now needs to be nurtured and rewarded. Customer service people now need to *stop* catering to customers' whims and individual needs. This will surely mean some retraining as well as some personnel changes. You will also need to bring on board people who can analyze current systems for delivering products and/or services to customers and redesign them to create as much customer satisfaction as possible for as many customers as possible *without* customization.

- ### *Reconfiguring the entire organization*

Back in the Jungle, each organization's hierarchy was fairly flat, and information generally moved through it sideways, from one unit, function, or team to the next. A Warrior organization, however, cannot function efficiently with such a structure. A traditional top-down hierarchy needs to be established, though for the sake of efficiency, it should have as few levels as possible.

Systems that are useful in the Jungle are built to react to customer needs and problems. The whole organization is oriented toward the outside so that it can fight to gain and retain each customer. The people who designed and built these systems were asked to work from the outside in (i.e., from customer needs and desires) when designing them. These systems give a great deal of authority to the people who work with and most clearly represent the customer.

Warrior systems, however, must be designed from the inside out, beginning with system needs and then working toward the customer. The intention is still to create a positive customer experience, but the primary force behind the system is to make it efficient and speedy. As a result, the customer gets the product as easily and quickly as possible and as close to the way they want it as the system can provide. However, the organization must now produce as much of the product as possible, as quickly and efficiently as possible.

Normally, this means a complete overhaul of internal systems and how they function and interact. However, in some cases, managers with a Hunter mind-set may be able to lead the way toward *mass customization*, which uses Warrior-style systemization and automation to produce each product unit to the individual customer's specifications. Dell Incorporated, for example, has Pioneered a system that allows the customer to specify what characteristics they want in their computer and receive a finished product off the assembly line within forty-eight to seventy-two hours.

- *Learning to do business side by side with competitors*

Survival in a Jungle market is usually a zero-sum game: the more you gain, the more your competitors lose, and vice versa. In a Battleground, however, you will need to learn to do business side by side with many other large consolidated companies. Indeed, in Battleground markets, it is often true that the only way to survive is through collaboration with the competition.

A sports bar chain, for example, needs to be able to offer a variety of major beer brands, not just one; yet for each beer company, the chain offers many important points of distribution. No major brewery

can afford to give up this market, nor can the chain afford to offer
only a limited selection of big-name beers. Furthermore, each big beer
manufacturer has a stake in the chain's success. Instead of trying to fill
this niche alone and keep competitors out, it is to the benefit of each
big brewery to share this piece of the market.

In practice, this is usually more of an accommodation than it is a
collaboration. Rarely do the competing organizations actually work
together or even talk with one another.

Sometimes this accommodation is nothing more than a process of
feeling out the competition. For example, an airline may raise prices
on certain routes to see what its competition will do. If other airlines
follow suit, the company will keep its new prices. If its competitors do
not, however, the airline will usually reset prices at their former levels.

Solutions

- *Change the focus from customer satisfaction to speed, volume,
  and efficiency*

In a Battleground, speed, volume, and efficiency are paramount.
This applies to the movement of products, but it applies just as much
to making changes to the organization itself. An organization-wide
reinvention initiative must be quickly established and communicated to
everyone in the organization. The nature of the required change must be
presented clearly, unequivocally, and in multiple ways so that people can
quickly sign on or make plans to leave. Managers and employees need
to very quickly understand the new structure of centralized decision
making, the new driving forces in the organization, and the reasons
behind them.

Changing the targets to speed, volume, and efficiency helps in a
number of ways. It becomes a rallying point (and a source of buy-in)
among managers and employees, it enables systems to be redesigned to
eliminate anything that slows down (or adds unnecessary expense to)
any process, and each of the three targets becomes a potent and tangible
symbol of all that is new about the organization.

Change efforts, and any discussion of them, should focus on process
rather than structure. As will eventually become evident, as you identify

the key processes in each business and redesign those processes for speed, volume, and efficiency, the issues of decision making and management will automatically be confronted and dealt with.

- *Change the leadership immediately to a council of generals*

The most powerful way to illustrate any major change desired by management is to appoint people who understand and epitomize the behaviors and attitudes needed in the new system. This is particularly important if your company needs to make the difficult and drastic change to a Warrior organization. Key decision makers (including, in many cases, some or all the people at the very top) need to be replaced as soon as possible. The new leaders must be comfortable making decisions, giving orders, and taking full responsibility for their results. They must also understand that the big picture is crucial because the company now operates in a realm where survival is predicated on selling large volumes of products that earn small margins.

- *Cut off any movement toward anarchy*

When Hunter companies come together to form a new Warrior corporation, there is a natural tendency for the individual business units to try to retain and exercise most of their autonomy. This can become very destructive very quickly and can even lead to something very close to anarchy.

To keep this from occurring, top management must move very quickly to build linkages among groups, units, businesses, and their leaders. Strategic leadership needs to be provided as soon as the Warrior organization is created so that there is little or no disruption in business and a firm foundation is created for the new Warrior culture.

Adaptation Issues

Doing business in the Jungle has meant continuously cutting costs while at the same time maintaining or improving the level of customer service. This provides excellent preparation for the kind of cost-cutting discipline needed in a Battleground. In fact, because it is no longer necessary to focus as much attention on the customer, more energy and attention can now be directed toward reducing costs to their absolute minimum.

Thus the transition from a Jungle market to a Battleground market is not as difficult to make as many others. There will, of course, be some redundancies in any merger or acquisition, and these will need to be eliminated. Infrastructure systems—e.g., inventory control, order entry, and accounting—will need to be aligned; this can be a complex and difficult task when the systems are very different and must be totally redesigned.

During the realignment of key systems, there will need to be a change of power. In part, this means that many top managers will need to be replaced. It also means that the locus of informal, everyday power must change as well, from marketing to operations and finance.

This repositioning needs to be led by the new CEO, who will probably be the only person able to supercede the top managers from the old systems. The CEO's central dictum should be that the old rule ("the customer is king," an external measure) no longer applies; in its place is a new rule ("highest speed, most volume, lowest cost, and highest quality," all internal measures).

The human resources department also needs to be very active in pointing the way for the new culture, especially among management. Hunter-style managers must be asked to leave and should be given severance packages appropriate to their contributions in the Jungle. New positions will need to be created, and new people with Battleground experience should be brought in. The new culture must be defined and disseminated to all the consolidated parts. New reward systems need to be put in place as well.

The new culture needs to be clearly defined and widely understood and accepted. (GE, for example, has a massive training program that inculcates managers with the principles and values of the company's culture. The CEO spends time with each group to help them understand how the culture functions. This indoctrination—and it is truly an indoctrination—resembles military training programs; its purpose is to help people understand how important following orders is to the survival and profit of the company.)

HR will also need to be involved in most of these consolidations in other ways. It will need to handle any layoffs and to complete and manage any due diligence efforts required prior to the merger or acquisition. HR should also be involved in defining the likely effect of the consolidation on the culture, predicting the kind of resistance that will take place, and devising programs that will help make the transition as smooth as possible. This strategic activity should continue for quite some time, from the initial due diligence report through the organization redesign and all the way to full implementation of the plan.

Becoming a Warrior organization also means learning to coexist in the market with other major players like yourself. It means letting go of the win-lose model of competing for customers in the Jungle. In a Battleground market, *all* the major players are winners—it is just a question of who wins the biggest.

You must now make sure that your products are differentiated in some way from those of all the other major players in your market. Then you need to construct marketing and advertising programs that win the attention of the customer for a while so that you can experience a volume increase.

Your competition will do the same when your program hits the field, so there is a kind of tug-of-war here. To get a sense of how this works, observe the marketing and advertising activities of companies like Nike, Reebok, Pepsi, Coca-Cola, Burger King, or Wendy's. Immense marketing attention is paid to the customer, yet in no case is a substantial new benefit provided. The key is simply that the customer's attention is drawn to the company in a positive way. Some customers will be sufficiently attracted to change whom they do business with, at least for the duration of the program.

Your new Warrior company, following the strong lead of its CEO, needs to very quickly establish to management and employees that it is no longer operating in a Jungle environment. People throughout the organization know who their customers are, where to find them, and how to get to them. But now they must also be taught that they cannot capture the entire market or, in most cases, even half of it.

In a Battleground market, there is a tacit agreement that the market will be shared and, in many cases, that the very same customers will buy from two or more competitors. How many of us are truly loyal to FedEx over UPS or one brand of computer disks over another? Consider the videotape market, in which the difference between competitors' products is effectively zero. Each major producer controls about 10 percent of the market. A lot of hoopla is created around each brand name and each level of quality, but the average consumer will never notice any actual difference in performance among the different brands or levels.

2. **Drift into this market from a declining Kingdom.**

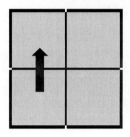

After dominating the market for some time as the premier producer of a product in high demand, your company finds that the product has become a commodity and is now produced equally well by a handful of competitors.

Once a company has established itself as a Ruler in a Kingdom market, there is a tendency for its managers and employees to assume that this is its rightful, God-given place, yet the Kingdom is never the final phase in a product's natural life cycle. Your company may be able to create a Kingdom market and protect its position through patents, marketing strategies, and/or the elimination of all meaningful competition. But eventually—after some months, years, or decades— *every* Kingdom market erodes into a Battleground. This may be because a patent runs out or because some company with huge capacity and resources decides to enter the market, thus creating significant competition.

In either case, your company is now faced with a very different market environment and must either learn how to do business in a Battleground or get out of the market entirely. This is roughly akin to learning that the inheritance you've lived on all your life is suddenly gone and you've got to get a job like everyone else.

Imagine that the people in your company have gotten used to its Ruler status. All of you are used to focusing your attention on *answering the phone*—that is, on responding to the incessant growth in demand for your product by upgrading facilities, constructing new plants, hiring more people, innovating new versions of the product, and increasing prices to meet these needs. New versions and variations of the product come out every now and then to keep customers demanding more and more. The product has been a provider for the company, usually for a long period of time (sometimes for fifteen to twenty years). The margins it has created have been used to weather storms in product areas that are more vulnerable to changing market forces. Infrastructures have been built around the research, production, and marketing of the product. These have been allowed to grow in size to handle ever-increasing demand. Product innovations have become more and more difficult, so the research departments have become large and costly. Production processes have either been allowed to deteriorate, or huge investments have been made in new equipment. Sales forces are large and deployed deeply in many territories. Because of the product's success, people connected with it have received many rewards, which they wish (and in some cases expect) to continue receiving. Leaders in this product area have become strong political forces by being chosen to lead more and more significant portions of the company.

Eventually, however, the phone no longer rings as often. There is too much capacity in the plants. New units sit on the shelves unsold. Other companies have taken away some of your customers with lower prices or better service or product modifications or some combination of these. Customers continue to need your product, but your company no longer has a stranglehold on the market.

The party is over, and management knows it; yet because everyone has gotten so used to their Ruler status, parts of the organization are in turmoil. There are impending layoffs, and a new focus on efficiencies needs to be created in all parts of the system. Discretionary funds for conferences, meetings, trips, new offices, etc., have dried up. People in the organization no longer are clear about what their roles are and how they are expected to contribute. The manufacturing people want to see more orders and more product going out the door, but the orders continue to decline. Marketing people dream up multiple projects to bring in more customers, but the customer base keeps shrinking nevertheless. Research and development people are busy creating what they consider new and improved products, yet these are not well received by customers. The financial people call for more and more discipline in spending but find that all the activity to improve manufacturing, marketing, and R&D is actually costing more. The rest of the supporting cast is equally confused.

Welcome to the inevitable last phase in the life of a product, where it is very competitively priced, of uniformly good (or at least adequate) quality, and easily and readily available from several sources. Your organization must now either make the huge, difficult, and disruptive change from a Kingdom to a Battleground market or else get out of that market entirely.

In many cases, this second option—selling the product license, the unit, or the entire company—may well be your best strategy. Indeed, often there's a very good reason why your company has been knocked off its throne: the organizations that have forced you into a Battleground market can do a better job than your company can with this product. In such a situation, it's probably time to get out of that particular business. Accept that your company's run of success with this product is over. Formally celebrate your past success, honor the people who helped create it, and move on. In many cases, this will create the least disruption to people's lives and lead to the best bottom line, especially if you can sell out for a substantial sum.

In fact, most companies that have attained Kingdom status choose not to continue with a product once the Kingdom market erodes into a Battleground. The disruption is simply too great, the required change too radical. Seeing that the organization's infrastructure simply cannot withstand the impact, management wisely decides to sell out to a competitor.

For example, 3M invented videotape and ruled that market for some time, extracting significant margins of between ten and twenty dollars per cassette. In the early 1980s, however, the company's patent ran out, and several competitors, some of them Japanese, began producing the product. There was some price erosion, but 3M kept its retail price at around ten dollars, using its brand name to help support that price. In the mid-1980s, however, Memorex suddenly cut its price to about four dollars. At first, 3M's management figured it was a marketing ploy to secure the customers, run 3M out of the business, and then raise the price again so Memorex could make profits. But then other companies matched Memorex's price, and it soon became clear to 3M that it was not a ploy and that its competitors were actually making sufficient profits at that reduced price.

3M decided to stay in the business and to do battle with these companies on these new terms. After all, management reasoned the company had made huge capital investments in its manufacturing processes, and its leaders felt that they could bring their costs down and pay for those investments while still making some profit. However, as 3M began to come close to the new price, its competitors continued to reduce theirs.

In order to keep the division alive, top management cut costs inexorably and downsized the division far beyond any cuts the company had ever made. There followed several years of excruciatingly painful working conditions for everyone involved in that part of the company.

3M's problem was that it was a Ruler organization trying to quickly learn to adapt to the ways of a Warrior. Meanwhile, it was faced with competitors who were much more adept at operating in a Battleground market. They were Warrior organizations that know how to win under these conditions. Finally, after ten years, 3M gave up the videotape business, unable to even sell off its assets. The division simply could not change deeply enough and fast enough to compete in a Battleground.

All Ruler organizations face similar difficulties if they attempt to do business in a Battleground. If your management does decide that it wishes to compete in its new Battleground market, your company's entire culture of abundance and domination will need to change. The organization must become frugal and willing to share the market with other large players. The focus of all activity must change to efficiency, speed, minute margins, small product adaptations, and developing and maintaining extremely high volumes. In the meantime, do not be surprised if a buyout offer comes on the table as one of your competitors seeks to absorb your company to serve its own efficiency and volume needs.

In many ways, the demands of a Battleground market are exactly the opposite of those of a Ruler culture. As a result, people who were performing very well before according to certain guidelines may become very frustrated with the 180-degree discrepancy between what they have been trained to do and what they are suddenly being asked to do.

Key Issues

Cleary, the central issue is whether to continue to compete at all or to create a strategy for bailing out. Unfortunately, either decision will be traumatic for most of the people in the company. The only other option is more traumatic still: make few or no changes and ride a death spiral to bankruptcy. (Sadly, this is exactly what does happen to many companies.)

If your company does choose to attempt to profitably compete in this new Battleground market, it will have to go through some significant and painful downsizing as well as an overall restructuring of both the work and the organization. And as if this won't be difficult enough, the power structure of the company may be laced with people who have ties to the product's history. These people are going to be very disappointed when they watch their pet projects of many years simply disappear.

It may, perhaps, come as no surprise to you that most efforts to adapt a Ruler organization to a Battleground market are unsuccessful. The companies typically become dysfunctional and financially unsound and are usually swallowed up by competitors, often after at least one reorganization.

Common Difficulties

- *Coping with the new reality: survival*

As the Ruler of a Kingdom market, your organization may have seemed invincible and capable of almost anything. Now the very structures that supported your dynasty will weigh on your organization like a huge stone about its neck. Virtually all the old culture—habits, practices, proclivities, processes, attitudes, etc.—is no longer needed and, in fact, now gets in the way.

To put it simply, your organization must change enormously and extremely quickly or else die. Everyone in the organization needs to very quickly understand this. This means that a huge internal communication effort must immediately be put in place, and it must come from the very top.

- *Garnering buy-in for a major change in the way almost everything is done*

The slow-moving enterprise of the Ruler now needs to become known for speed. The old luxuries and discretionary resources are gone (or must go), probably forever. The company can no longer be driven by a focus on the growth of its assets; it must now focus on huge volume and be satisfied with minute margins. The old emphasis on internal politics, in which leaders of the different units competed with one another for prominence and accession to the throne, must give way to a single centralized command, whose orders must be followed to achieve fully coordinated strategies.

None of this can take place by fiat or executive order, no matter how powerful and charismatic your organization's leader may be. There *must* be widespread buy-in for every one of these changes or your organization will expend much of its resources shooting itself in the foot, over and over.

- ***Creating a new and alien culture and finding the right people to lead it***

Nothing short of a total transformation of the organization is required. Few, if any, of the organization's top people will be able to make this transition. Given the change that is needed, this is a simple fact of life; it does *not* represent a failure on the part of either the affected people or the organization as a whole.

One painful reality is in the disappointment of those who have, for years, performed successfully, learned all the rules, and developed all the political skills needed in the Ruler environment. Now the rules need to change drastically, and the political skills that were once so valuable have become serious detriments to the organization. Another is that the kinds of behaviors needed to be speedy and Spartan have not yet been developed or supported; indeed, they are probably totally foreign to your company's current managers.

- ***Ensuring that the change is complete, swift, and all-encompassing***

The transformation from Ruler to Warrior must not only be thoroughgoing; it must be swift and irrevocable. By definition, there will have been little or no preparation for the change. Essentially, the whole organization must be pushed off the dock and then quickly taught to swim.

Within a few weeks, there will need to be severe downsizing throughout the entire organization, especially in management. Those managers who do remain must quickly learn how to do things without lengthy discussions about when and how they should be done. If they cannot make this adjustment quickly and reasonably smoothly, they will need to be replaced.

Solutions

• *Rid the organization of everything not absolutely necessary to production and be 100 percent public about it.*

It can take years to completely realign a culture developed by a Ruler organization. Nevertheless, if you are competing against companies that are already functioning as Warriors, you must move as fast as possible because until most of the transition is complete, those companies will consistently outperform your own organization. (This is one of the main reasons Ruler companies that suddenly find themselves in a Battleground market often let themselves be bought out rather than face a lengthy, difficult, and painful transition.) Even though the full realignment will take some time, your company can probably be saved if you promptly begin making substantive changes and continue the process steadily and vigorously.

There will be shock, panic, and resentment no matter what you do, but these can be kept to a minimum by *immediately and fully* disclosing to everyone in the organization exactly what is being done, why it is both necessary and unavoidable, and what they each stand to gain and lose in the process. There is no upside and an enormous downside to withholding information or plans from employees in this situation. Buy-in is possible only in an environment of total, honest disclosure. You will still lose some of the people you hoped to keep but far fewer than if leaders play their cards close to their chests.

Once news of the organizational redesign has been made public, the very next move is to excise as many layers of management as possible. This quickly streamlines the organization, saves a considerable amount of money, demonstrates to employees that the redesign effort is for real, and sends a message throughout the company that managers no longer make up a privileged class. This effort should be swiftly followed by the following changes:

- The massive research enterprise that develops (or searches for) new products should be shrunk by 40–80 percent because most of this function is probably no longer needed.
- The overstaffing in most departments that existed to keep everyone informed, involved, and rewarded should be cut back, again, by 40–80 percent.
- The great majority of project managers in marketing are no longer needed and should be reassigned or let go.
- Any element of production that can be efficiently automated should be and the relevant jobs eliminated.

All these people served important functions in the Ruler system, but they will be detrimental to the speed and leanness now needed to survive in the new Battleground.

If your primary competition is a company that has primarily operated in a different Kingdom market but has recently entered your own market and successfully managed to take away a significant chunk of your own market share, then the time crunch may not be so urgent. Your competitor is probably faced with similar concerns and may also need time to plan and implement its own realignment. The same is true if your primary competitors have recently entered the Battleground from the Frontier. But if you are facing competition from companies that have considerable experience succeeding in either a Battleground or Jungle market, your company is already in a state of emergency. Everyone in your organization needs to know this, and they also need to understand that the only hope for survival is swift and drastic measures.

In essence, your company, which has been used to feasting during a time of plenty, must be put on a crash diet. Furthermore, the benefits of this diet—a long, healthy life for the company and long-term job security for those who survive the downsizing—need to be sold internally, over and over, with great vigor and even greater sincerity.

None of this, however, should be taken as a mandate to recklessly downsize and create ostensible efficiencies through ruthless or capricious decision making. (Exhibit A is "Chainsaw Al" Dunlap, who is primarily known not for brilliant leadership but for his penchant for reckless downsizing.) All the changes recommended in this chapter need to be made in such a way that managers and employees have the support they need to go through the change process with their integrity intact. Otherwise, to put it bluntly, why even start?

Nevertheless, the final result must still be fewer employees, fewer managers, much less cost, quicker processes, an orderly work process, and a product or service that contributes to the lives of vast numbers of customers. This makes the job of designing and implementing the change process truly monumental.

- **Create a new culture based on the centralized issuing and carrying out of orders.**

With few exceptions, this can only be done by removing the person at the top and bringing in someone with experience as a leader of a Warrior business. There simply is no time for the current CEO or president to learn all the ropes of leading a Warrior organization. Your company needs someone who can very quickly establish the vision of a Warrior organization and put the pieces into place over as short a time as possible.

Furthermore, as soon as this new leader arrives, they need to issue something very close to this proclamation: "In order to survive, we need to reinvent ourselves from top to bottom, and we need to do it fast. From today on, our focus is on creating as many efficiencies as possible everywhere we can. Without these efficiencies, we lose money on everything we sell, and the greater our sales volume, the greater our loss. As part of this focus on efficiency, your new mandate is not to consult with many of your colleagues before acting but to follow the instructions you receive from above as swiftly and efficiently as you can. We must all reinvent how we work if we are to continue to compete." This message needs to quickly permeate the whole organization.

- **Redesign all key processes.**

Although this necessary change can be easily stated in only four words, it is usually a massive effort. Leaders and other important people in every department need to put their heads together to redesign all your organization's processes around the steps needed to accomplish them.

This means eliminating all variances at the source of every problem. It also means reducing or eliminating the involvement by everyone not absolutely necessary to any department's core process.

Furthermore, this needs to be done quickly—in months rather than years and ideally within a couple of quarters. This will send enormous shock waves throughout every part of the organization, so tell everyone to expect them.

- *Realign the entire human resources function.*

Although all departments will need (and should be expected) to streamline, the human resources department will require a full-scale realignment. For some time, the department has been supporting a culture that is no longer viable; quite naturally then, many of its key people are as entrenched in the old system as the managers they have served. HR's selection process, review process, and reward systems all need to be redesigned, probably from scratch, to reflect the new realities in a Warrior company. Your primary considerations will be these:

1. *Attraction and recruitment of prospective employees.* You should no longer be looking for the best of the best. Instead, simply look for the skills actually needed to carry out the orders of management and perform the functions of the work.
2. *Selection and hiring.* Management now needs to select only those people who will fit well within the new culture.
3. *Orientation of new employees.* It is essential that new people understand, immediately and clearly, the importance of getting things done speedily and without any unnecessary hesitation or deliberation. In a Battleground market, there is no time for much discussion or for the reassessment of goals.
4. *Training and development.* Management must make it clear that people will now be trained only for the work that needs to be done and any specific future work that is clearly foreseen. Employee development efforts should now become minimal.
5. *Performance measurement and development planning.* The principal issue now should be whether people carry out the imperatives of their jobs and the orders of management, not

whether they have shown innovative tendencies and purposely broadened themselves.

6. *Career development.* Future managers should be clearly recognized, designated, and developed according to a concise and forceful plan. Everyone else should be judged mainly by their accomplishment of the clear objectives formulated by management.

7. *Compensation systems and formal and informal recognition.* These should reflect management's imperatives of developing speedier and higher quality systems and *increasing production and sales volumes.*

A more macroscopic HR issue needs to be dealt with as well. In Ruler organizations, human resources departments are often politically very strong. When the whole organization culture system changes, it is critical that this political force be reconstituted. Top management needs to move swiftly to reshape the department's role and functions.

HR should now fulfill almost solely an administrative role rather than a developmental one as well. Reporting requirements will need to change so that top management can have more oversight and more direct control. In many cases, some or all the hiring should be moved out of HR and into the specific departments. Understandably, the people in HR are going to strenuously resist such efforts, which means that the mandate for change in the department needs to come directly from the very top level of management, if possible, from the CFO or CEO. Furthermore, in my experience, the required changes can only be made if a new HR director is brought in. This person should, of course, have considerable experience as an HR leader in a Warrior organization.

Adaptation Issues

- *Leading the change from the very top*

The change process should, at minimum, be aggressively supported by your company's board of directors. It's better still if the process is *driven* by the board since the CEO will almost certainly need to be replaced. (The exception is if the current CEO is new *and* has significant experience leading a Warrior organization.)

From the very top of the organization, develop and communicate a *radical* new vision of the company that includes what it will look like if it is successful in its new market environment. Work to get commitment from every part of the organization; as needed, replace people who do not completely buy into this vision, then lead the organization to this radical goal.

- ***Engaging the help of change management specialists who are familiar with this kind of change***

Do not expect your own OD people, no matter how talented, to be able to provide all the necessary expertise and experience. A good outside consultant can help your organization to avoid all kinds of strife and a host of common mistakes.

- ***Understanding the disruption to people's professional and personal lives that will be created***

Because the required transformation will be so enormous, at various points, all the various stakeholders in the organization—from employees to top managers to directors to stockholders—will lie awake at 3:00 a.m. and ask themselves, "Is it all worth the incredible personal strife that's been created?" If the effort ultimately results in the company's long-term success, then the answer is "probably." But if the company becomes a marginal player or can at best only manage breakeven each year, then the answer is "probably not."

Obviously, each organization has to create its own answer to this question. Still, a decision to stay in the market should be made only if the clear consensus among key leaders and directors is "we think it will be worth it, and we're committed to doing our best to make it work." In the absence of such a solid and unanimous (or nearly unanimous) commitment at the very top, it's usually best to close up shop.

This is not a situation where it makes sense to say "Let's give it a try and see what happens." Other approaches that won't work include arrogance ("We've got a great team here, we'll *make* it work"), false optimism ("Things will get better if we can just hang on for the next two years or so"), and outright denial ("We can't let go of the people who have given us so many years of their lives. Besides, Michael Moore will skewer us in the media"). As we all know, when reality squares off against good intentions and fond hopes, reality always wins.

Ultimately, your top leaders will need to go back to the organization's mission and ask, "Which direction will best help us continue to fulfill our mission?"

If you do decide to proceed with the adaptation effort, everyone at the top needs to be ready and willing to live with the fallout of replacing key people, including the CEO, the HR director, and other powerful (and usually entrenched) leaders. The process will very likely result in many angry or disgruntled employees.

Some of the people who will need to be let go will be on the verge of being vested in their retirement programs (vest them anyway). Others will be new hires who left (or turned down) great jobs elsewhere; some may have relocated to join your organization. (Give these people good recommendations and decent severance packages.) Still, others will be talented people aged fifty and older who may have a hard time finding new jobs. (Make sure that they get honest recommendations, appropriate severance pay, and reasonable sums of money for retraining.)

- *Managing the downsizing process thoughtfully and compassionately*

Remember Chainsaw Al Dunlap. If the process is handled poorly or harshly, the new culture will reflect the attitudes formed by the survivors of the downsizing. Often, these people suffer from anger or severe depression, and many feel guilty about remaining employed while others have been downsized. These attitudes are ready to surface at the first hint that things are going poorly or that management doesn't give a damn.*

- *Considering each division separately*

If your organization has a division that has routinely turned significant profits, which the company as a whole has used to solve problems elsewhere in the organization, an additional concern will need to be addressed. People at the top of the company need to be told that they cannot reasonably expect the same large profits in the future and, in fact, that they should expect minimal profits or even losses for the next one to three years while the division reinvents itself. Top management then needs to figure out how to function effectively without this income.

In some cases, a single division of a company may move from a Kingdom market to a Battleground while the rest of the organization continues to operate in Kingdoms. In such a case, this division must be structurally separated from the rest of the organization and reinvented while the structure of the rest of the company should remain unchanged.

- *Never losing sight of the fact that becoming a Warrior organization is an enormous and difficult job*

Change management consultant Daryl Conner is fond of saying that unless a change is absolutely necessary, don't make it because it is much more difficult than anyone imagines in the beginning. This is especially true of the change needed to transform a Ruler into a Warrior.

- *Knowing when to stop*

The new CEO needs to steadily monitor the ever-present drive for efficiency and leanness and to put the brakes on if it begins to create organizational anorexia—e.g., if all or part of the company is in danger of becoming too lean to function effectively.

In addition, the top leader needs to recognize when even the best efforts at redesign and efficiency are not making the organization (or division or unit) sufficiently competitive. If this does become clear, the CEO needs to have the courage—and sufficient support from the organization's directors—to say "Enough is enough. It's time to sell or close."

Neither of these decisions can be made easily nor can they be made without very high-quality information. Thus, the CEO's management team should be charged with regularly providing the kind of information needed to make these difficult calls.

As you weigh all the factors involved, beware of getting stuck in product pride. It may feel satisfying to declare "It's our product, and it defines who we are. How can we possibly sell it off to someone else?

Either we find a way to make a profit with it or we go down with it, like a captain and their ship." Ultimately, however, such a position will harm virtually every stakeholder.

It also helps to remind yourself and your colleagues that consumers don't care who makes your product. As long as the product itself doesn't change, no one gives a hoot whether it comes from you, your competitor, Nabisco, Ford, Procter & Gamble, or some nineteen-year-old's garage.

Although I have made much of the difficulty involved in transforming a Ruler into a Warrior, a significant number or organizations have made the change successfully. Here's how one organization I consulted for pulled it off:

The general manager shut down his entire operation for two weeks and took all managers on a retreat. There, together, they developed a new vision for the organization. Each manager was then assigned a team of employees. The ultimate charge was for each manager and their team to change some significant part of the organization and its operations.

During the retreat, each manager was also asked to create and present a detailed plan for how they and their team would accomplish the needed change. When each manager presented their plan, it was thoroughly reviewed, critiqued, and refined by the other participants.

After the retreat ended and the plans were implemented, daily and weekly meetings were held to provide support and monitor progress in terms of specific numerical goals. The plan was to stop the bleeding first then change the organization's structure and all its key processes within six months. The general manager led the process at all levels, but by design, the change effort involved every single person in the organization.

And the effort paid off. Within a year, the organization was turning a profit again and functioning as a successful Warrior.

All this demonstrates that while making the transition from Ruler to Warrior is as tough as training a lapdog to herd sheep, it can be done.

CHAPTER ELEVEN

Becoming a Ruler Organization

A Ruler's primary concerns are (1) being the only company to deliver desired products to eager customers, (2) watching out for potentially serious competitors, and (3) constantly working to increase the value of its products and services.

However, though many organizations strive for Ruler status, it is a rare and fortunate company that achieves it. This status is usually accomplished through a combination of hard work, innovation, smart decisions, good timing, and luck. Only a very small percentage of businesses ever become Rulers; indeed, in today's business world, there are not a great many Kingdoms left.

A top-down, strongly managed organization is necessary for successful operation as a Ruler. With such a structure, management can make sure that products get to customers on time, that sufficient innovation occurs and is properly funded, and that the competition can be routinely defeated or bought out.

When a company emerges as a dominant force in its market, it will get the best results by adopting a Ruler culture. However, organizations that have attained Ruler status find themselves faced with a difficult choice: either grow—sometimes quite significantly and quickly—or lose domination. Although growth is a sound strategy, there is a limit to how large and powerful management can become before size itself becomes a problem. After a certain critical mass has been reached, the company's size and unwieldiness can slow down its ability to produce and deliver products, satisfy customer demand, and achieve high margins.

This is the bind that many organizations found themselves in during the 1980s and 1990s. They had built up empires that had simply become too large. Suddenly, they discovered that their smaller, leaner, more adaptable competition was bearing down on them. Margins shrank dramatically. Mass downsizings followed as companies were forced to adjust.

Paradoxically, the other danger a new Ruler organization must strive to avoid is thinking and acting too modestly. A Ruler cannot stay in control of a Kingdom market for long unless it consistently makes bold moves to innovate and squelch any serious competition. Ruler managers should not be satisfied with gaining small percentages in market share for such marginal gains are no longer significant. Instead, Ruler managers should be charged not merely with winning skirmishes but with slaying dragons—i.e., totally vanquishing potential competitors.

Managers in a Ruler organization need to learn to use all their substantial resources to conquer or purchase any real competition. They need to learn how to go for knockouts instead of higher scores. A good Ruler manager should not be content until the competitor is gone or at least not in competition on as strong or threatening a basis anymore. In short, managers need to start asking a good deal more of themselves and the people who report to them.

In this chapter, we'll examine the three ways in which companies can move into a Kingdom environment and what they need to do in order to thrive as Rulers in each situation. These three ways are the following:

1. *Conquering and leaving the Frontier*—your new product has been a success in the Frontier and enjoys a patent or some means of marketing or distribution that no one else can duplicate.
2. *Escaping from the Jungle*—as the result of your successful manipulation of a product, product line, supply chain, and/or marketing channel, you pull away from all other competitors and achieve market domination.
3. *Taking control of the Battleground*—through smart and aggressive marketing, you wrest the great majority of market share from the last few competitors in a Battleground market, or alternatively, your company simply acquires some or all of the remaining significant players.

Here's what these three variations look like on the market grid:

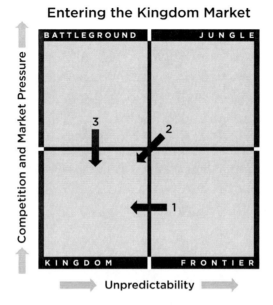

Entering the Kingdom Market

Let's now look more closely at each of these three situations and at what you and your organization can do to obtain the best results in each case.

1. Conquering and leaving the Frontier

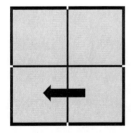

Your new product has been a success in the Frontier and enjoys a patent or some means of marketing or distribution that no one else can duplicate.

When your product is a hit and your organization has developed a means of keeping others from successfully competing, several important things need to happen:

First, prices must be set high, at the limit the customer is willing to spend. (Cell phones, for example, sold for about one thousand dollars each when they were first introduced, and the charge for airtime was also very high.)

Second, because of the resulting high margins, your company can now afford to aggressively develop, modify, and innovate products. This is what enables it to continue to stay ahead of its competition.

Third, these margins provide the financial resources to support the development of a top-down, strongly managed organization. Building and successfully operating this infrastructure provides significant financial rewards and incentives for management in a somewhat restrictive and paternalistic environment.

Key Issues

The road that transforms Pioneers into Rulers will look familiar because you'll remember it from a Marketing 101 class. This road is the traditional S curve that illustrates the life of a product from initial investment through productivity to decline.

Life of a Product

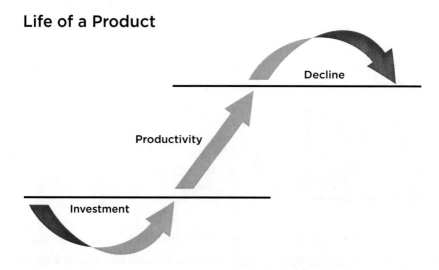

Every new product goes through an initial period of development, during which heavy investment is needed in order to bring it to market.

If it makes it through this period, it then enters a phase during which it has the greatest potential for bringing returns to its investors and producers. During this time, there is normally the heaviest demand, and the key organizational problem is filling that demand.

Eventually, however, competition catches up, and profits begin to decline. By this time, some kind of renewal strategy (e.g., the rollout of a new product, the significant redesign of the old product, the opening of new markets, etc.) should be in place. As an organization follows this S curve, there is the widespread expectation that the resources expended in development will be more than adequately repaid during the period of productivity. This is exactly what happens when a product enters a Kingdom market.

The most common mistake new Rulers make is focusing their attention almost solely on fulfilling orders and forgetting that those orders will eventually begin to dry up. In the midst of the productivity stage, it is easy to believe that no one else will be able to enter the market as a major competitor. In fact, however, longtime Rulers have stayed successful precisely because they committed substantial resources to protecting their territories and keeping others out. This means paying close attention to competition and other external market forces. (The people in charge of this should be quite near the top of management so that any threats will be taken seriously and dealt with immediately.)

New Rulers must also quickly learn to walk an unexpected tightrope. On the one hand, they must stay ahead of competition by creating innovative variations on their products and/or by extending those products into new areas. On the other, these efforts must not draw off so many critical resources that order fulfillment is affected.

Kingdoms are maintained by a tenuous alliance that is built entirely around the customer's ability to procure the highly desired product. Therefore, keeping customers should always be the number one goal of any Ruler organization. This means carefully and consistently monitoring delivery to ensure that it is on time, accurate, and otherwise satisfactory.

Finally, there is the issue of control. Although the word *control* has some negative connotations, the fact is that control is an essential ingredient to the success of a Ruler organization. A Ruler that underutilizes control and power in dealing with competitors (and attempts at regulation) makes itself too vulnerable to outside forces.

Of course, overutilizing control with customers and employees is just as much of a problem: it creates dissatisfaction and unnecessary complications.

Furthermore, employees and customers appreciate Rulers' use of control, provided that it is used for their benefit. America Online's customers, for example, appreciate the company's ability to make special deals with a variety of retailers but only to the degree that those deals benefit them as customers.

Common Difficulties

- *Managing the cultural change*

The key problem in moving from the Frontier to a Kingdom market is changing the culture from an open, loosely managed system to one in which management sets a variety of controls and boundaries. Most entrepreneurs find this too confining and restrictive. They simply are not able to develop the confidence that these processes are in their best interest. These changes inevitably take away freedoms that existed in the Frontier, and they are naturally met with resistance, shock, and even outrage. If this transition is not handled intelligently, serious morale problems can arise, and these can sabotage the entire organization's performance.

- *Continuing to meet customer expectations*

The new Ruler must also take care to retain the essential values of its product or service. It behooves the company not to undermine those key attributes that customers or dealers have learned to rely upon.

Because the focus of a Pioneer-turned-Ruler tends to shift somewhat away from research and development and more toward getting product out the door promptly and reliably, there is a temptation to pay less attention to quality. This is a mistake, however. The new Ruler instead needs to learn what product qualities (and/or other customer expectations) are particularly valued and focus on maintaining these. If he does not, the organization may find itself slipping quickly back out of a Kingdom market, either into a Battleground or, worse, a Jungle. As an example, Frontier organizations often take responsibility for all unsold product on dealers' shelves. If it is not sold within a certain time, the company takes it back and issues a credit. In contrast, Ruler organizations are sorely tempted to ask dealers to absorb the cost of any unsold product. In certain circumstances (e.g., in cases where a product is very well protected against competition by patents), this may be acceptable. But in most situations, a refusal to accept returns may simply encourage dealers to stock competing products or work with other suppliers.

- ### *Reducing internal friction*

A third type of difficulty can arise when two or more new Rulers exist as parts of the same large organization, with each Ruler dominating its own market. Without careful planning and oversight, each Ruler can become its own little empire, and these empires may not work smoothly together within their larger organization. The more levels of management that are created and the smaller the span of control each individual manager has, the more encrusted these empires can become and the more time and energy must be allocated to make the larger system work.

While an overt, vertical hierarchy remains essential to Rulers' success, this hierarchy should therefore contain only as many levels as are strictly necessary and no more. In addition, structures and devices need to be put in place to create cooperation across boundaries. For instance, your company may create a variety of product manager and process manager positions to represent cross-functional interests. Another common solution is to create teams to support efforts to cross boundaries among regions, functions, technologies, etc. All these cross-functional positions and teams must be developed from the top down, however, with clear, strong support from the highest levels of management. Otherwise, they are likely to be ignored.

- ### *Setting healthy boundaries with customers*

A final challenge for new Rulers is setting boundaries in terms of what the organizations will and will not do to please customers.

Early on, many Frontier organizations learn to never say no, to be willing to do whatever the customer, distributor, or retailer wants in order to get their business. When a product is first making inroads into the market, this total *can-do* approach is often wise. However, by the time a company has become a Ruler, this bending over backward loses the organization more than it gains. What was once an admirable focus on the customer then becomes a lack of discipline that puts a drain on the bottom line.

Obviously, Rulers still need to please their customers and deliver high levels of customer service, but wise Rulers will negotiate (and if necessary, renegotiate) these boundaries with customers in advance, making it clear precisely what they will and will not do. Once these agreements are in place, the Ruler company then needs to set up a system to monitor and maintain those boundaries.

Solutions

• *Establish a climate of openness and trust.*

People who have worked in a Pioneer organization share a clear vision that they were part of a developing company. Together they built a culture of innovativeness, responsibility, and accomplishment around that vision. They believe very strongly in both the vision and the culture.

When it is time to begin building a more permanent and powerful business to take over and control competition, some of the core pieces of this culture need to change. There needs to be less reliance on individual ideas of how things must work and more reliance on systems that work every time and in the same way. There now needs to be less concern for the innovativeness of the technology and more concern for efficient production and control.

To managers used to (and loyal to) a Pioneer culture, these changes may feel like a stab in the heart, a signal that their opinions are no longer considered as valuable. They may feel (perhaps quite accurately) that they will be less able to be themselves in this new culture.

In general, the cultural changes your organization will need to make will not go down easily with most of the people in it. Many will feel that management has betrayed them and sold out, that the company's most positive attributes have been discarded. (There is some truth to this last item, though what has been discarded is a set of values that the company has outgrown.)

Therefore, it is critical that all the things we know about managing change be brought to bear in assisting people to make this very difficult adjustment. Indeed, the attraction (and the thrill) of becoming a Ruler often blinds management to the fact that enormous changes must take place, both for the organization and for the people in it. This makes it all the more important to make good use of best practices for dealing with change.

- *Redesign your processes to focus on both efficient delivery and customer satisfaction.*

Rulers must change their focus from pleasing customers at virtually any cost to getting as much product out the door as efficiently as possible while still meeting customers' key demands. This means identifying (and if need be, creating) the most effective and efficient processes for meeting all delivery goals. It also means learning what truly matters to customers (and what, therefore, must be maintained) as well as what customers aren't especially worried about (and what, therefore, can be dispensed with).

- *Manage people benevolently and honestly.*

Without vigilance and a strong moral commitment from its top managers, Ruler organizations can easily deteriorate into power systems that do not take people into account and focus entirely on financial concerns. How to avoid this temptation? Leaders, especially those at the top of the organization, need to maintain and model honesty and integrity at all times. They also need to make it clear that such behavior is highly valued in employees' dealings with customers and with each other. The flip side of this is that managers who don't value, practice, and encourage integrity must be encouraged to find new employers.

Ruler companies all have the opportunity to become more than just business organizations earning profits. They can learn to benefit all their stakeholders for a long time once management understands clearly that the purpose of business is to provide valued products and/or services to customers and to do so with integrity. Making money is not the purpose of a company but an outcome, a result to be striven for. Reminding managers and employees of this helps to avoid the dishonesty and lack of integrity that we so often observe in business life.

Leaders should also go beyond what is merely necessary to establish good will with employees. This might mean investing in bonuses, raises, gifts, awards, appreciation programs, etc.—though it might also be as simple as regular meetings or lunches with employees.

- ***Establish early warning and quick response systems.***

Rulers can easily become obsessed with production and filling orders since they are where the profits are. Furthermore, there are considerable problems just in making sure that enough products get produced and sold. As a result, managers in a new Ruler organization tend not to be easily influenced by information outside the realm of production and delivery. They simply do not want to hear about other problems.

Unfortunately, potential competitors become very envious of businesses that realize excellent margins, and they will not allow those businesses to exist without a challenge for very long. It is essential, therefore, that at an early date you put systems into place that scan the market horizon for potential incursions by competitors. These scouting systems need to be properly funded and staffed. Furthermore, they need to have a direct line to top management or they will go unheeded by mostly everyone.

- ***Develop cross-functional mechanisms that enhance the effectiveness of the hierarchy.***

In twenty-first-century Kingdom markets, Rulers cannot afford to relax and foster internal dynasties. Neither a horizontal nor a siloed structure will work for Rulers. In order to achieve the greatest efficiency and effectiveness, your organization will need a clear hierarchy augmented by many cross-functional and (perhaps) cross-market mechanisms.

For example, as certain markets get more demanding, the parts of your company that service one particular market (or a certain group of buyers) may decide to create an overlapping business mechanism that reaches across those parts and unites them in serving that particular market or set of buyers more effectively and efficiently. For instance, your industrial heating-and-cooling company might create a cross-functional system (often called an overlay business) to specifically address the needs of hospitals or airports or heavy industry. In a Ruler organization, however, this overlay business must always be less important than the core business.

- **Communicate and support a clearly defined business strategy throughout the organization.**

Ruler organizations function best when they develop a clear strategy for doing business as well as clear guidelines for all managers and employees to follow. This explicit sense of direction provides everyone in the organization with a sense of freedom, focus, and meaning.

Two important caveats apply here, however. First, if you want to help focus and energize your employees, you must have a full-fledged business strategy in place, not just a set of sales or profit goals. Second, that strategy must be clearly—and regularly—communicated (and recommunicated) to everyone in the organization. New hires should understand the strategy clearly by the end of their first day on the job.

Most Ruler organizations today relate all operational decisions to one (or more) of four to five key strategic initiatives and expect departments to arrange their objectives similarly. Without this clear connection of plans, activities, and strategy, department activities quickly deteriorate into uncoordinated action, resulting in organizational anarchy.

- **Actively discourage bureaucratic behavior.**

Although Ruler organizations are bureaucracies, they should be highly functional ones. This means actively encouraging managers and employees to share ideas with one another, make suggestions, ask questions, and communicate frankly and honestly. It means encouraging mutual respect regardless of anyone's rank or job title, and it means actively *dis*couraging behavior that gets in the way, such as the following:

- Saying "it's not my job" and turning away rather than making an effort to locate the right person

- Wrapping oneself in the cloak of the organization—e.g., writing "the company has made the decision" instead of "I decided"
- Dodging responsibility or trying to foist it on others
- Butt covering
- Protecting one's turf
- Brownnosing

As soon as possible, some mechanism should be put in place to flag dysfunctional management behavior so that it can be corrected or eliminated quickly before it can become a way of life in the organization.

Adaptation Issues

As your organization crosses the line from Pioneer to Ruler status, keep in mind the following:

- ***Grow slowly, even reluctantly.***

Despite appearances, growth of an organization is not *ipso facto* beneficial, yet Ruler organizations tend to grow automatically, with little or no effort, at least at first. Therefore, one of top management's concerns should be carefully monitoring growth and, as necessary, reining it in, stopping it entirely, or spinning off one or more pieces of the organization. Wise managers focus not on mere growth but on careful, deliberate, well-managed growth.

Too much growth too fast can cut deeply into margins, wreak havoc with cash flow, and create a chaotic business climate in which the speed of change outstrips people's ability to cope. Remember too that management is responsible for anyone laid off because of excess capacity.

- ***Focus attention on those markets that can be dominated.***

It may appear that Rulers, with their high margins and relatively secure positions, can afford to take significant risks in new markets and with new products, yet experience teaches us that this is not the case at all. While Rulers may have the financial stability to weather a string of poor decisions or tough breaks, *no* organization can afford to take a significant risk when the risk-benefit ratio does not make good business sense.

Your company's focus now needs to change. As a Pioneer, you focused on creating new products and garnering a reasonable market share. Now, as a Ruler, your focus needs to be on maintaining your dominance in current markets and expanding into other markets only if you can extend your domination into them.

A good example here is General Electric, which won't even enter a market unless key people in the company believe it can become either number 1 or 2 in that market.

If you do wish to continue to develop and market brand-new, first-of-their-kind products (and thus remain in some Frontier markets), then you'll need to set up a separate division or unit—with, of course, a Pioneer culture—to do this.

- *Improve the collection of information about your customers and competitors.*

As a Pioneer organization, you probably collected (and made good use of) information about product acceptance and use. While you certainly need to continue doing so, you must now *also* regularly collect information about competition, market shifts, and market volatility. This information must quickly be made readily available throughout the organization, especially to people at the top.

- *Keep innovating.*

A danger for all new (and many not-so-new) Rulers is believing that answering the phone and delivering product are all that need to be done. (As your people will discover, it takes a great deal of effort just to do this much right when you're the Ruler of a Kingdom market.) However, your retention of Ruler status is very much dependent on the amount of continued innovation (in both processes and products) that your company supports.

2. Escaping from the Jungle

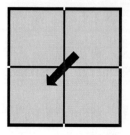

As the result of your successful manipulation of a product, product line, supply chain, and/or marketing channel, you pull away from all other competitors and achieve market domination.

On occasion, a company in a niche market that has been struggling against heavy competition finds the right mix of acquired or merged companies, functions, distribution systems, and finances. This enables the organization to overtake all its competition and become the Ruler in a new Kingdom market.

This is what happened with AOL Time Warner, which put together the necessary ingredients to dominate the new communications market. By stringing together operations in film, cable TV, music, book and magazine publishing, broadcast syndication, online services, and other parts of the communication industry, the company has developed a formidable force in a number of markets.

Making a leap from the Jungle into a Kingdom is both difficult and rare, but it can be done. Almost invariably, a series of mergers or acquisitions is required. For example, as I write this chapter in the summer of 2001, the German media conglomerate Bertelsmann is attempting to turn the book publishing industry (which has been a Jungle for nearly two hundred years) into a Kingdom that it can dominate. Its strategy is simple: acquire one publishing company after another.

Making the jump from Hunter to Ruler status requires a major qualitative change. Typically, this means gaining control of some part of the distribution or supply chain. Red Lobster became the country's ruling seafood restaurant—and a model for many subsequent national restaurant chains—by making large-scale deals directly with big fishing fleets around the world and flying the product directly to their restaurants each day rather than buying stored, refrigerated fish from wholesalers. Red Lobster also Pioneered the use of teams in organizing waiters who, together, make sure the customer's experience is first rate.

Key Issues

• *Refocusing the business*

Once a new organization has been created via mergers, acquisitions, and/or alliances, management must turn its attention to creating a new focus for that new company. No longer should such a high value be placed on retaining customers through attentiveness to their every desire and need. Instead, the focus needs to change to delivering high volumes of what you are sure the customer wants.

This does not mean that the customer is no longer important (although the change of focus may give that impression to many of your Pioneer managers). It does mean that everyone must learn to build and rely on systems (rather than individual decisions and initiative) to take care of customers and to do this with far more transactions than before.

In this new environment, it is easy to lose the customer voice in the millions of transactions that occur. Just trying to fulfill burgeoning demand is difficult enough. Customer satisfaction remains important, but it should no longer be the paramount concern.

This change is one of balance and emphasis, not a complete reversal.

• *Building systems across the whole organization*

You will need to very quickly design and build systems that work across the business units of the new organization. This will be expected by customers, who do not care how big you are or what friction exists between the parts of the organization. If they cannot get their desired products in the places and manner in which they want them, they'll perceive it as your failure to perform.

In a Ruler culture, leaders of the functional parts (such as marketing, manufacturing, and research) hold positions of significant influence in business decisions. These high-ranking people will need to work together smoothly in order to meet the needs of customers and make a good profit. This cooperation is both critical to success and very difficult to achieve. (Not achieving it is precisely the reason why some organizations fail to hold on to their Ruler status for very long.)

Working effectively together then needs to be an organization-wide goal supported both by (1) some internal mechanisms that force cooperation and (2) goals and rewards set by management that reinforce such cooperative activity. For example, consider companies whose divisions often share the same customers but offer them different products. In such organizations, management would be wise to establish a sales group comprised of people from all the different divisions who serve a particular customer or set of customers. Other such mechanisms might include councils that represent the interests of marketing or manufacturing across division lines.

Furthermore, all the units in the company need to be brought together into a form that can be used to effectively rule the relevant markets. Your organization will need to develop and implement a variety of systems to ensure that all parts work together in sufficient harmony to enable the company to succeed against potentially powerful forces. You specifically need to avoid having a series of separately organized units, each with its own infrastructure, all competing for customers (and thus gradually losing ground in the market).

Common Difficulties

Ex-Hunters who become Rulers face many of the same issues discussed in the first section of this chapter, in which Pioneers must learn to act like Rulers. However, Hunters have some additional concerns and issues as well.

When your organization moves out of a highly competitive environment with tight resources to a dominant position with adequate resources, at first, your people will feel like they have died and gone to heaven, but they will pull their heads out of the clouds once they realize how difficult it is to continue to dominate a market over time and how much effort is required to sustain a culture that encourages and supports such domination.

In order to make the transition to Ruler status, the old culture of achievement, flexibility, and strategy must be replaced by one that focuses on profit numbers, management oversight and control, and successful use of power to maintain and grow the market. Such a culture may seem arrogant, power hungry, and unbending to someone who has excelled in a Jungle.

Furthermore, people who feel that they have at last escaped from the intensity of the Jungle will soon discover that they are, at most, half-right. Yes, the specific demands of the Jungle may largely have fallen away, but Ruler markets are no less intense; they are simply fueled by very different concerns: fulfilling ever-increasing customer demands and generating consistently high profit levels.

Going from Hunter to Ruler is one of the toughest transitions that managers and employees can make in a twenty-first-century market. The issues of leadership, values, human resource management, and organizational structure all become quite important as well as emotionally charged. Significant resources and effort must be invested in helping people to make this transition and replacing those who simply can't adapt.

I use the word *must* in the previous sentence quite deliberately. This investment cannot be avoided without incurring some serious consequences. Unfortunately, many companies, caught up in the excitement of securing a dominant position, tend to overlook the human and organizational problems that naturally result. These corporations thus unwittingly hinder their own success (and their smooth transition to Ruler status).

To underscore this point, let's consider the different roles played by managers and marketers in the two types of organizations.

Hunters	*Rulers*
• Aggressively create loyal customers by attending to their every need and whim	• Aggressively restrict consumer choices and meet only the critical ones
• Value customers for their loyalty and patronage	• Value customers for their potential to increase demand and profit and help the company grow
	• Demand the highest prices the market will bear

It is not easy to inculcate these unfamiliar Ruler behaviors and values into employees and managers who may view the old Hunter values as morally superior.

One common and particularly thorny problem results when the consolidation, acquisition, or merger of a number of Hunter organizations transforms a market almost overnight and creates a new monolithic Ruler organization. Such mega organizations tend to be unwieldy, and forming the right kind of structure at the top is a complex and difficult task. On the one hand, it is critical to establish solid and reliable central control; on the other, it is just as critical not to stifle the productive and creative energy within any individual unit.

Solutions

The solutions suggested in the Pioneer-to-Ruler discussion are very pertinent here. When Hunters become Rulers, however, the solutions that follow should be considered as well.

- *Develop a comprehensive business strategy.*

Typically, a group of Hunters get pulled together through mergers and/or acquisitions into a new, multifaceted Ruler. When this first occurs, the individual units (and of course, the managers and employees in them) will be confused about their roles in the new system. Although this will cause some resentment and anxiety, this is entirely natural and, indeed, unavoidable. Nevertheless, those emotions must be addressed promptly—the sooner the better—by top management.

As quickly as possible—ideally before all the mergers or acquisitions are completed—people at the very top of the new mega organization need to craft an organization-wide business strategy. This strategy should acknowledge and use the varied knowledge and talents of all parts of the new company. This means

- helping key people quickly become familiar with all the units and divisions of the newly structured organization, including the products, histories, missions, customers, markets, major successes, and cultures of each;

- clearly communicating how the different parts of the new organization will fit and work together;
- creating and clearly communicating organization-wide business goals; and
- if necessary, creating a new mission statement and/or corporate vision statement.

It is all too easy for organizations' missions to be forgotten (or at least partly unfilled) during a merger or acquisition. The consolidation itself is so engulfing and complex that management can easily lose sight of the essentials. As a result, managers often jettison their organizations' original mission and settle for what they feel they can wrest from the chaos around them. This is another reason why it is so important to quickly develop a focused, authentic mission and clearly—indeed, vociferously—communicate it to everyone. In fact, this is one situation where it makes sense to deliberately overcommunicate by repeating the same key messages to everyone in the organization over and over using multiple media—e-mails, hard-copy memos, meetings, posters, displays, etc.

To a large degree, the exact configuration of the new organization should grow out of and support the new strategy, goals, mission, and vision. This means that the individual units or divisions should more or less be left alone until these overarching concepts have been developed; otherwise, your people may be faced with the demoralizing prospect of one reorganization after another. Yet this hands-off period cannot go on for too long—certainly for no more than six months or so—or your people will be equally demoralized by the uncertainty.

- ***Immediately begin using the resources of the new organization for innovation.***

Wise leaders in new Ruler organizations are keenly aware of the opportunity to create new products from the new relationships that have been created. They make a point of quickly developing processes to identify key capabilities throughout the organization, bring them together in supportive ways, and encourage them through concerted management action. This sets the stage for long-range domination of the market.

- ***Resist the temptation to immediately and significantly downsize.***

Your stockholders and other people with their eyes primarily on financial concerns may want to make as many visible gains as possible in the short run. They would have the company shed people and take all the losses right away in order for it to create profit gains as soon as possible. But don't rush into such actions thoughtlessly.

There will be obvious areas where redundancies occur, and there will surely need to be downsizing in those areas. However, allow some time to pass and observe how the organizations learn to merge and work together. This will provide you with a clearer view of what the new system needs to look like, and it will help you to avoid the all-too-prevalent practice of reducing headcount only to build it back up again. Learning how the different units work together creates opportunities for interesting innovations in products and/or processes.

When leaders succumb to the temptation of the short-term bottom line and quickly rid their companies of seeming redundancies, they seriously undermine the opportunity for creative synergy. Furthermore, the message is given out that the merger or acquisition was really about immediate profit, not about strategy, long-term development, and market domination. Is this the message you want your stakeholders to hear?

Only after the new organization is up and running fairly smoothly is it time to look for redundancies and overlaps that indicate a need for fewer resources. I should add that, in my experience, the issue of redundancy is less significant in Ruler organizations than in Warrior organizations.

This is not to say that all jobs should be considered sacred. Some minor bloodletting may be necessary, even at first, particularly when one of the newly acquired units is overstaffed or when one has a history of poor performance. But handing out pink slips like party favors in order to quickly boost the bottom line ultimately serves no one.

- ***Build a new identity.***

People who have been part of a Hunter organization usually feel a strong allegiance to it—and justifiably so because they have worked hard for it to succeed in a very difficult market environment. Now, however, their allegiance needs to be focused toward both their original company *and* the newly formed one.

People at the top of the new organization thus need to create an overarching corporate identity that

- gives meaning to all the different parts;
- unifies the parts into a single, consistent whole; and
- positions the functions and departments that need to lead the organization so that they have sufficient influence.

This task is often difficult, and it is always very important. The better a job top management does with it, the more energy will be created and applied and the less resistance there will be at all levels.

- ***Avoid overpoliticization.***

A Ruler organization runs on the good will that is created among its parts as well as on the leadership of its CEO (who, in essence, is a benevolent king or queen). This requires the building and sustaining of good relationships, which in turn requires a culture that rewards discussion, negotiation, and active listening. However, in the very legitimate interest of getting things done, people in a newly formed Ruler organization can very quickly become absorbed in taking sides and forming coalitions. Soon, despite (and indeed partly because of) everyone's best intentions, the organization can become immersed in political infighting. In fact, it is not uncommon for people who were quite cooperative and friendly in their Hunter organizations to quickly become enmeshed in politicking and infighting once their companies become parts of a larger whole.

While there is no simple or across-the-board solution to this problem, much of the infighting can be avoided if management

- exercises strong leadership;
- creates, implements, and clearly supports and communicates a solid strategic plan;
- defines and communicates clear goals and expectations;
- provides strong, steady involvement of top managers in each of the units and divisions; and
- demonstrates the desired openness and teamwork at the top.

There's a personal component to this as well. In companies that are new to the world of domination and large profits (e.g., those with stock options and profit-sharing plans), people suddenly see the potential to get rich. They then work long and hard to become positioned to share in the organization's success. Management needs to formally recognize these efforts as supporting the organization as a whole as well as by advancing individual business units. Furthermore, it must be careful not to overreward individual initiative and performance or it will only encourage a dog-eat-dog culture.

Adaptation Issues

Since the move from Hunter to Ruler status normally takes place quite quickly, and since most merged or acquired Hunter organizations have been in existence long enough to have their own entrenched cultures, the adaptation issues are both significant and thorny. Here are some ways to successfully manage the change:

- *Be patient and careful with Hunter managers and employees.*

People who are used to a Hunter culture will have great difficulty understanding the need to get management approval on a regular basis. They will not be able to easily tolerate what looks to them like unnecessary bureaucracy or even outright power-mongering. Therefore, from the highest levels down, management needs to help people to understand the benefits of increased coordination from the top. People at all levels also need to know that while a larger bureaucracy is now necessary, everyone benefits from one that is *no larger* than necessary. These messages will probably need to be delivered over and over with patience and understanding.

It is, of course, crucial that these messages be reinforced with genuine (and genuinely useful) information. Even the slightest hint of "oh, don't you fret about it, we in management know what's best" can inspire a mutiny.

- *Use the hunting knowledge of people in the organization to minimize the bureaucracy.*

Although your organization is now a Ruler, this doesn't mean that management should forget the lessons its divisions learned in the Jungle, such as understanding and attending to customers' issues. Use Jungle wisdom whenever and wherever it can be helpful, especially in keeping bureaucracy to a minimum.

It is a swift road back to the Jungle, and forgetting the customer—or indeed, ignoring any of the important lessons learned in the Jungle—will bring competitors out of the woodwork quickly.

One of my favorite top managers made it a practice to ask people he met in the hallways what they had done to reduce the amount of unnecessary bureaucracy in the organization. He listened carefully to what they had to say and put the best suggestions into practice, and guess what? They worked.

- *Carve out places in the new organization for Hunter leaders to exercise their influence.*

The aggressiveness that had been rewarded in a Hunter company can be turned into either a negative or positive force in the new Ruler organization. There is a tendency among top management to replace Hunter leaders with more profit-focused people. *Resist this tendency* and, instead, give the best Hunter leaders positions of significant power and influence. Also make them accountable for profits, however.

Hunter managers who find themselves in Ruler organizations often get the idea that profit *is* the purpose now even though they believed differently before, but a Ruler's focus on profit does not change the fact that organizations are in place to serve customers. I am continually amazed by the number of people who truly believe that the purpose of business is profit. Unfortunately, Ruler companies tend to promote that erroneous view, and it is easily learned.

3. Taking control of the Battleground

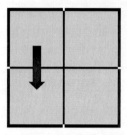

Through smart and aggressive marketing, you wrest the great majority of market share from the last few competitors in a Battleground market, or alternatively, your company simply acquires some or all the remaining significant players.

Battlegrounds are always difficult to survive, let alone thrive, in. If your margins consistently erode for a year or more and there seems to be no way to stem the tide, the product or product line (or even the entire business) simply may no longer be viable. In other cases, a product's usefulness or demand may steadily decline to the point where something significant must be done.

Typical strategic responses to such situations include the following:

- Trying to increase the perceived value of the products
- Lowering prices
- Attempting to enter new markets in the Jungle or, occasionally, in the Frontier, as Hewlett-Packard has done

Occasionally, however, a company will put together a series of moves that nets it a ruling position in a Kingdom market. Usually this involves one or more mergers, acquisitions, or strategic partnerships. As I write this sentence, Ford has begun implementing a gutsy and ingenious plan that it hopes will transform the company from a Warrior to a Ruler. Ford is well aware that consolidation in the auto industry is occurring at a rapid rate as cars become more resilient and useful for longer periods. The business of selling new and used cars thus has become difficult to grow since the business of replacement is steadily slowing.

Ford has decided to address this problem by acquiring the ability to provide owners of all makes of cars with tires, after-market parts and supplies, light engine maintenance, collision repair, auto insurance, and parts recycling (i.e., auto junkyards). The company is working aggressively to do this throughout the world and, thus, to dominate the industry as the foremost full-service car company. Instead of sharing the new and used car market with Daimler-Chrysler, GM, and the dozen or so Asian and European companies, Ford hopes to set itself apart as the premier source of everything connected with automobiles. The company would, in effect, become king of the hill by redefining the products it markets and the customers it markets to. Ford will soon compete on an unequal basis with the after-market companies, tire replacement shops, the auto accessories stores, the minor repair facilities, and the body shops throughout the world. As Ford implements its strategy, it will face off against all these smaller companies, all of which are, of course, vulnerable to price erosion and limited in their financial resources. Ford believes that, at some point in the future (though it may be decades hence), Ford will have accumulated a critical mass under its corporate umbrella, at which point it will be able to rule the market and set prices more or less as it wishes. If Ford succeeds, it will find itself in the enviable position of being able to control margins on a wide variety of products other than cars.

In terms of overall culture and structure, there is probably a closer likeness between Warrior companies and Ruler organizations than there is between any other pair of archetypes on the grid. Warriors and Rulers both have generally vertical structures and, therefore, are no strangers to bureaucracy and top-down management. Both types of businesses are driven by volume, and both are deeply involved in managing access to their products.

However, Warriors are concerned primarily with constantly increasing their number of sales outlets or access points; in contrast, Rulers want to limit and control them. Warriors share shelf space with a few competitors; Rulers want to be the only one on the shelf. (When possible, they will try to own the shelf itself.) These are crucial distinctions, and they have profound cultural and organizational ramifications for companies that need to make the transition from Warrior to Ruler.

Key Issues

After years of living with small margins and needing to sell millions of units in order to create worthwhile profits, managers in a Warrior-turned-Ruler organization will usually heave an enormous collective sigh of relief. They feel that they can at last relax a bit and take a few breaths. However, very quickly, a new sort of vigilance needs to be put in place. Your organization will need to be ever on the lookout for other players that hope to make inroads into the market and take over the Kingdom.

While it is by no means easy to knock a Ruler organization off its throne, this can and does happen. In fact, it is not unusual for a competitor to quickly (sometimes within a few months) acquire the ability to deliver a product similar to the Ruler's at a significantly lower price.

This is exactly what happened in the early 1980s with the videotape manufacturing business. At the time, 3M had ruled this market for several years. Then suddenly, Japanese-made video cassettes started appearing on shelves around the world. They had the same standard of quality but were only one-third the price. 3M management thought this was a ploy, that manufacturers could not make money at that price and that they would eventually have to raise their prices. But 3M was wrong. It soon became clear that a new manufacturing process had been developed in Japan, and as a result, Japanese companies could make a tidy profit from their cut-rate cassettes, provided millions of people bought them—and of course, millions did. By 1995, 3M was entirely out of the videotape manufacturing business, and its Kingdom market had reverted to a Battleground.

Warriors are traditionally concerned with getting access to as many different points of sale as possible. When they attain Ruler status, however, they must learn to expend an equal or greater amount of energy and resources on undermining potential competitors wherever and whenever they emerge. Similarly, in a Battleground, an organization responds to heightened competition by fighting harder, pushing for stronger sales, more points of distribution, and greater market share. As a Ruler, however, it must learn a different form of aggression. A Ruler organization can most effectively deal with market encroachment by temporarily undercutting competitors' prices, luring away their most valued people, and buying up competing organizations outright. The success of such efforts depends, in part, on continued vigilance and the ability to strike immediately when signs appear that a serious competitor wants to enter the market.

Warriors live by a few essential doctrines. One is *volume*, another is *lowest possible cost to us*, and a third is *brand value*. As a Warrior transmutes into a Ruler, however, these corporate values need to change, and the changes will not happen automatically. They need to be carefully planned, implemented, monitored, modeled at the top, and supported on all levels.

First and foremost, the value of lowest cost to the company needs to be replaced with *highest price acceptable to customers*. This value will drive many decisions and activities in the organization, including a commitment to support the innovation necessary to merit a higher price.

Volume should remain important to a Ruler but in the context that there should be a never-ending high demand for the company's products. Volume now needs to be induced not only by ever-increasing points of distribution but also by the regular introduction of new forms of the products. These new product versions, in turn, must be backed by significant innovation or, at least, enough innovation to increase customers' desire to secure any new forms of the products.

Microsoft's office products are an ideal example. Though Microsoft advertises continually, it does not make the same huge advertising investments that, say, Warrior companies such as Nike or Miller Brewing do. Microsoft also makes sure that each version of each of its products is sufficiently new to customers to keep them coming back for more. (It is a function of a Kingdom market that customers keep buying those new versions in huge quantities even when they are rife with bugs and glitches.)

Another substantial cultural change that needs to be made involves people's attitude toward innovation. In a Battleground, innovation is basically about appearances. By definition, the product is a commodity that varies very little from one manufacturer or producer to another. The way to grow and retain customers, therefore, is to appear different enough to get them to choose your brand over the others. Innovation in Battleground markets thus tends to be about appearance, convenience, or perceived effectiveness, not about new products or even a significant change in a product. (For example, consider Daimler-Chrysler's two new offerings, the Prowler and the PT Cruiser; they are perceived as very innovative even though they do not offer any real technical changes and, in fact, are totally retro in style.) Indeed, a significant innovation can even cause a product to move out of the Battleground and into a Jungle, thereby requiring a change in the organization's whole approach and culture.

But as your company takes its place as a Ruler, the rules change. The very reason your organization has become a Ruler is that customers perceive its products to be significantly different from (and better than) all its competitors. This perceived difference is the key to the company's future success, and therefore it must be carefully and thoroughly nurtured.

Now that your company has attained Ruler status, its primary objective is to *keep* its products from becoming (or at least being perceived as) commodities again, things that are available from more than one source. This means that you can no longer think of new packaging or configurations as innovation. Your company has to get very serious very quickly about innovating by offering significant changes in its products; furthermore, it must provide the resources necessary to create and support such innovation. This means, among other things, enhancing each product in such a way that your customers feel a need to buy the new versions because they think that it will provide them with something that actually works better.

Lastly, the allocation of resources in your organization will need to change dramatically as you assume the mantle of an industry Ruler. The amount of authority, status, and clout wielded internally by the functional departments (marketing, sales, manufacturing, research, etc.) will also need to change by increasing quickly and dramatically.

In a Warrior company, these functions all share the same goal: to move as much product into the hands of customers as quickly, efficiently, and expeditiously as possible. This very goal needs to be substantially altered if your corporation is to maintain its Ruler status. The new goal should be for each function to become the best in the industry. Each should exist in its own right, with its own mission and goals. Each needs to be strongly supported by all levels of the organization, especially at the very top. This means allocating human and financial resources to each department at levels that would be unheard of in a Warrior organization. It also means having much higher expectations of each department: each should be expected to grow steadily stronger and to add ever more value to the organization.

However, depending on the type of products your company produces and the industry in which it does business, one particular function should be the most influential. All functions are *not* (and should not be) created equal. For example, manufacturing companies will (and should) have more influence coming from manufacturing or engineering. Pharmaceutical companies will naturally be heavily influenced by marketing and/or research. (Usually, some tension arises regarding the amount of influence these functions have, and often considerable political jockeying takes place because of it. All this activity, properly handled, can eventually create the energy needed to get products to market in a timely fashion. Handled poorly, however, it can slow down the processes of innovating and selling.)

Common Difficulties

Making the change from a Warrior culture to a Ruler culture means steering through several rather difficult transitions. Your company will need to create new skill banks, new organizational structures, new power systems, and really, a whole new approach to business.

Here are the more specific dilemmas that your organization is likely to face:

- ***Replacing the goal of maintaining or growing market share with the goal of continuing to dominate***

Rulers don't (and shouldn't) share anything. They work incessantly to make sure there are no other serious competitors. They take no hostages. If they cannot dominate, they acquire. This attitude is quite foreign to employees and managers who have functioned in a Battleground, where sharing the market is one of the most basic facts of life. Everyone in your organization is going to have to make this big shift in viewpoint, attitude, and expectations.

- *Moving from lean and mean to strong and capable*

Warrior companies have cultures that are passionate about keeping costs down, so all the trappings that traditionally go with a Ruler culture, such as rewards for success and specific achievements, may seem extravagant, wasteful, or even foolish to some of your people at first. Yet now that your organization can afford these rewards, they can and should be used to motivate people to take on more and more leadership. In fact, in order for your company to maintain its Ruler status, it makes sense for it to spend whatever it takes to get the best of whatever it needs. Cost is no longer the issue; value to the organization is. In the past, focusing on low costs has meant compromising on other things. Now there is no need—and no good reason—to compromise when it comes to doing and being the best. (Of course, it still will be necessary to convince management that something is the best.)

But as a Ruler, your company needs to be fervent about pursuing its important goals even when this gets expensive. Innovation, for example, is very costly if you want to create new products that add real value to customers' lives. Acquiring the best minds is also expensive, but Ruler companies can and should invest in both as well as in keeping them away from potential competitors.

- *Changing the focus from small gains to big scores*

Warriors are rewarded for advancing markets by small percentage points and gaining incremental amounts of market share. In a Ruler organization, however, these kinds of gains should be considered trivial. Ruler managers should be rewarded only for knockouts—e.g., when a potentially major competitor is thwarted or gobbled up. This means not merely dramatically changing the reward system but getting your people to redefine their own views of achievement, success, and personal accomplishment.

- *Supporting a different kind of innovation*

Warrior organizations need to come up with ways to differentiate their products from the very similar offerings of competitors. They have to show how their products are different from—and better than—the other ones that everyone knows about. (Saturn, for example, invented a new way for customers to interact with dealers without hassles or haggling.)

As a Ruler, however, your company faces a different challenge. You need to show that each of your products is the *only* one around that does exactly what it does. The classic example here is Microsoft's Windows operating system.

Both of these types of innovation require talent, but they are worlds apart in what is innovated. In a Ruler organization, every innovation the company comes up with must create clear added value while a Warrior company simply needs to differentiate itself from the competition.

Once your organization becomes a Ruler, its big challenge is to create a culture that values and supports this added-value innovation. For many people in the company, this may mean making a big conceptual turn. Indeed, the very word *innovation* will need to be redefined as something that drives the company rather than as a form of product differentiation and market posturing.

At first, people throughout the company simply may not believe that all the new talk about innovation is anything but lip service. The expectations of your research and development department will change dramatically; the department will need new people, new thinking, and new skills. To the old Warrior people in R&D, management will seem to have gone mad. A similar perception may arise in sales and marketing if top management asks these departments to innovate the way the company's products are sold or distributed, yet it is crucial that management make and maintain a very serious commitment to this new, tougher, more expensive, and vastly more valuable type of innovation.

- *Managing as monarchs instead of as generals*

Because of their need to keep costs down and move large volumes of product, Warrior organizations need a military-style leadership and power structure. Management gives orders, and employees need to follow those orders without questioning, interpreting, or changing them.

But a Ruler organization cannot function particularly well in this way, just as a country run by a military dictatorship can never truly thrive. What was a military chain of command now needs to become more like a benevolent monarchy, with a king or queen, an inner circle of ministers, a collection of ministries, and a body politics. Similarly, leaders of a Ruler organization need to manage largely by generating collective political energy—that is, buy-in—rather than by simply issuing orders. This requires a huge change in the way both managers and employees think about leadership, roles, and their organization's culture. It also requires a whole new take on the meaning of time since getting this buy-in is a time-consuming task. (The issue of speed is not as critical for Ruler companies as it is for Warriors.) Such a change in mind-set can be made but never quickly, easily, or without a considerable investment of time, energy, and resources.

- *Fostering independence rather than dependence*

People who work in Warrior companies are trained to follow orders and move products quickly through systems. Decisions are made at the top, and everyone is expected to abide by them more or less without question. This arrangement will no longer work in a Ruler organization, however, since by its very nature, these behaviors stifle innovation, independent thinking, and creative problem-solving.

If your company is to make the transition to a Ruler culture, its people need to be given more flexibility in doing their jobs and more support for making case-by-case decisions. There may be times when a customer may be better served by breaking a rule or two. This would be unthinkable in a Warrior culture, and the errant employee would normally be punished or fired. Now, however, this type of behavior needs to be encouraged.

Some people in your organization will be intensely uncomfortable with this at first; a few may even feel it's a setup, a trick, or a test of loyalty. In addition, since Warrior organizations naturally attract people who like clear rules and black-and-white distinctions, and since such people have a particularly difficult time adapting, there will need to be some personnel changes. Unfortunately, this may mean getting rid of some of the company's most loyal and committed workers.

Executives and middle managers will have some serious adapting of their own to do. Essentially, they must learn—as Colin Powell and Dwight Eisenhower did—to become effective politicians rather than talented generals. They must learn how to create buy-in rather than demand compliance. (One general manager of a Warrior-turned-Ruler told me, with some pain in his voice, that he was under the impression that when his immediate reports agreed on something, that decision would then automatically move down through their departments. As a veteran Warrior manager, it was difficult for him to grasp that, in a Ruler company, important business decisions have to be systematically and carefully sold to people throughout the ranks.)

Solutions

It is absolutely critical that management understand that the transition from a Warrior culture to a Ruler culture simply cannot be made quickly or easily, no matter what consultants you hire and no matter how concerted your efforts may be. The scope of the change is roughly akin to transforming a military dictatorship into a benevolent monarchy. The success of such an effort will depend on having a wise and popular leader at the helm and on people's ability to stay focused and patient throughout the turbulence and discomfort of the change effort.

Here are some specifics that will help your company make such a change successfully:

- *Make good use of your Warrior ability to meet demand.*

As a new Ruler, your company's big challenge will be meeting demand. While this presents a variety of difficulties, your organization will probably be in pretty good shape because meeting large-scale demand in a Kingdom market is not that different from meeting demand in a Battleground. Indeed, many of the processes are similar. Because Warriors are particularly good at moving product to the customer, with some tweaking, this ability can be used to further dominate your market.

- ***Learn the art of raising prices effectively.***

As a Ruler organization, you not only can get away with raising prices but you will have to because you will need significantly higher margins in order to support the extensive research and development efforts that are now required. These R&D investments will pay off in significant innovation and creation of new, more valuable versions of your products, which in turn will increase sales.

But raising prices is an art, not just a technical skill. It requires careful research, proper timing, good judgment, and strong relationships with your distributors. Price-raising is a marketing skill that can be acquired only through practice and by taking significant risks. For this reason, do not depend on former Warrior marketers to miraculously develop these skills. Instead, bring in some experienced Ruler people to inculcate these skills in others.

- ***Build crucial resources.***

Take pains to ensure that every unit, department, and person in your organization has the resources it needs to do business well. A high standard of competitiveness and quality is necessary if your company is going to continue to dominate. Fortunately, your company can afford to do this because as a Ruler, it now has both the margins and the market share to pay for continued quality and performance.

Microsoft, for example, realized early on that technical people were its most important assets. Since then, they have gone to great lengths—some would say to extremes—to get the most talented people to join the organization. This has included hiring top-notch recruiters and setting up sourcing areas around the world.

It makes no sense for a Ruler company to cut corners. Getting rid of fat and dead weight is smart, but doing things on the cheap just to save a buck will only hurt margins or reduce market share in the long run. Your whole organization needs to go from lean and mean to well fed, well designed, and well managed.

Adaptation Issues

Managing the transition from Warrior to Ruler takes time, courage, money, and patience. It's a particularly complex transition because of the size of the organizations involved and the huge differences between them in how effort is focused and power is wielded. In particular, attend to the following:

- *Build a new overall identity for the organization.*

In order for groups with diverse organization cultures to come together, there needs to be a clear overall strategic goal that everyone in the organization can buy into and that everyone will be rewarded for achieving. In addition, people throughout the new organization need to forget about the power systems they have been parts of and build new allegiances and alliances that can hold the new system together.

- *Develop an overarching business strategy.*

For many companies, a business strategy is little more that a set of sales and profit projections for the coming year. This is particularly true of Warrior organizations since they live by cutting costs and increasing sales volumes. For a Ruler, however, such a bare-bones business strategy won't do since there is no longer such a bare-bones goal as moving as much product as possible as efficiently as possible.

In a Kingdom environment, leaders need to create a specific and detailed strategy that people throughout the organization can follow and rally around. Furthermore, in making essential choices about products, markets, investments, resources, and systems, it is important to involve as many levels of the organization as possible. This not only helps leaders to make wise decisions but also creates and supports cohesion among units, departments, and employees.

- *Set up vigilance processes.*

Counter-intelligence groups need to be set up to act as devil's advocates with the organization. Their job will be to surf the markets, investigate the competition, and look intently for where the organization may be vulnerable (or already in trouble). These counter-intelligence groups should report to top leaders, and their findings and recommendations must be taken very seriously (particularly at the highest levels) and communicated throughout the organization. This is quite a change from the typical Warrior attitude in which commands are issued and people are expected to carry them out without any questioning or hesitation. Strong leadership is needed to bring the ideas of this group to the front and to honor the people who bring them forth. Furthermore, it is essential that there be a visible way for these people to present their ideas and information without having them rejected because of political issues. Open forums for presenting and discussing such information can be helpful. I also recommend that people with serious internal clout be appointed to manage (or at least head up) all projects that result from such investigation, counterintelligence, and open discussion.

- *Lead the organization-wide change from the top.*

A Ruler organization simply cannot function effectively without a strong, highly visible, and widely respected king or queen. This person may be benevolent and may have a roundtable of trusted people to advise them, but they must still personally rule the organization.

An effective queen or king encourages employees and managers to develop loyalty and faith in the whole organization. They also personally oversee the entire transition process from Warrior to Ruler. As necessary, they should give extra attention to those parts of the new organization that may be in trouble (or that may be having a rough time making the cultural transition). It is crucial that none of this be relegated to a subordinate, no matter how much clout they might have.

In short, the leader of any Ruler company cannot be a financial analyst who lives by numbers. Intelligence is critical; so is the ability to explain, to connect, and to motivate. Charisma, while not an absolute requirement, is extremely helpful as well. Jack Welch at General Electric was a classic Ruler CEO.

The bottom line is that a CEO can make or break a Ruler company, and this is particularly true of a Ruler that is emerging from its longtime Warrior cocoon.

If there is any one crucial element behind becoming a successful Ruler organization, it is the ability of its key people to neither resist nor underestimate the all-encompassing nature of the organizational transition. The company's entire culture must be turned inside out and upside down. There will be resistance, fear, and very likely, outrage. But the enormous effort required is well spent nevertheless for when the smoke clears, your company will have transformed itself from a respected competitor to the market's one and only acknowledged leader.

CHAPTER TWELVE

Becoming a Pioneer Organization

Any organization that offers new-to-the-world products or services needs to operate as a Pioneer. Pioneers must be able to succeed in the very difficult circumstances created by Frontier markets, where much of what is encountered is new and unknown. Pioneers must gain a foothold in the marketplace while surviving the many unexpected and threatening events that inevitably occur when introducing new products or services.

Typically, Frontier markets involve new types of machinery, software, financial services, medical devices, online products and services, and so on. However, a Frontier market can also be created when an existing product or service behaves like a new one because of a major adaptation or improvement or because of a significant change in who uses it, how it is used, or how it is marketed or distributed.

One such example is urban car-sharing clubs in which a company owns a fleet of vehicles that it makes available at drop-off/pick-up lots throughout the city. Members typically pay a monthly fee to belong, plus a per-mile or per-hour charge for using one of the club-owned cars. This is a brand-new way of marketing a century-old product.

In the beginning, no one knows about a Pioneer's new product or service, no one sells or distributes it, there is no established channel for getting it to market, and there may not even be a fully developed process to produce it. Thus a Pioneer's primary concerns are

1. clearly *defining the business*—what it delivers, who it serves, and what effect it wants the new product or service to have on the world;
2. *building the needed resources*—capital, real estate, people, and technology—to create products and services that can survive in a Frontier market;

3. *creating quality, highly desired products or services*;
4. *making these products or services* known as new and worthwhile;
5. *developing the marketing channels* that can most easily and effectively distribute the organization's products or services;
6. *building an organization* that can bring products or services to market in a timely fashion, often in the face of inadequate resources;
7. *creating an organizational culture* that supports growth and innovation;
8. gradually *putting all the above elements into place* to create a profitable and sustainable business—i.e., figuring out what works; and
9. *managing the huge emotional and organizational stresses* that are part of functioning in a Frontier.

Innovation is the most central and distinctive quality of Pioneers. Managers in Pioneer organizations not only expect R&D people to come up with new products or services but also expect them to find a new and less costly way to produce and deliver them.

Perhaps the most important task of Pioneer managers is creating the circumstances and climate in which innovation can occur. (Compare this with the primary tasks of Battleground managers, which are to increase sales volume, add points of distribution, and reduce costs, or with those of the Ruler manager, which are to crush or buy out any serious competition.) This focus on innovation shapes many of the organization's decisions about people, space, management style, and the availability of research and development resources.

There are four ways to enter a Frontier market:

1. *As an entirely new organization with a new product, service, or product-service line.* You're an entrepreneur, and if you're lucky, you've got some investors or partners.
2. *From a Jungle, when an invention or adaptation puts your organization into a new market or channel.* You are part of an established organization that relies heavily on innovation to compete with other Hunters. However, you now have a new product or service that substantially changes—or will soon change—the way you do business.

3. *From a Battleground, when your organization decides to put resources into new-to-the-world products or services.* This is the rarest and most extreme of all organizational transformations, and I normally do not recommend attempting it.
4. *From a Kingdom, when your continuing effort to produce new products or services creates a new industry, product or service category, or marketing channel.* Here the challenge is to transform the Frontier into part of your organization's Kingdom before anyone else has a chance to create significant competition.

Here is what these variations look like on the market grid:

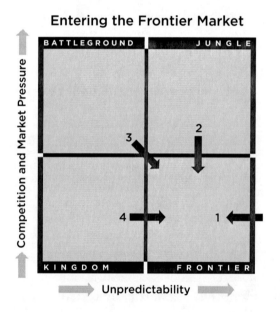

Now let's look more closely at each of these situations and at what you and your organization can do to obtain the best results in each one.

1. **Starting an entirely new organization with a new product, service, or product/service line**

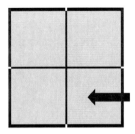

You are an entrepreneur who has developed a new product or service. Either you've got some investors or partners or you're able to start up an organization of your own.

Key Issues

Creating this organization will take lots of time, money, and people as well as new or cutting-edge technology.

Time typically seems to be the most readily available resource. However, this is an illusion. Indeed, it is critical to conserve time. If you take too long to get the new product or service into the market, or if you spend too long simply setting up the new organization's infrastructure, other forces will take over that will cripple your ability to make a profit. Many failed Pioneers began with very good products or services but simply ran out of time trying to establish themselves profitably in their markets.

Time must be managed very carefully through continuous strategic and short-term planning. *It is essential to focus the attention of the whole organization on the few crucial things that must be done well* even while everyone is fixing real and present problems that inevitably arise in a new market.

Money is normally a problem. Investment is usually needed to underwrite each major step in building the enterprise. The paradox is that while it takes money to grow, people often won't invest in your organization if it is not already growing.

People are the key to the success of the new venture. A Pioneer organization needs people with technological savvy to develop and improve products or services, people with the vision to guide that development (and the development of the organization as a whole), capable people to produce and sell the products or services, and committed people to form the infrastructure to support these functions.

While most business organizations need such people, the difference for Pioneers is that most or all these people also need to be entrepreneurial. Indeed, the more entrepreneurs, the better.

In most new Pioneer organizations, everyone tends to do everything; defined jobs, as such, often do not exist. Everyone may become a salesperson. Everyone may share in solving production problems; everyone may pick up some of the slack when support functions are understaffed (as is often the case). It pays, therefore, to have people who share the dream and are willing to make it happen however they can, including by playing multiple roles.

Savvy, committed people are also able to find ways of getting things done when there are few or no funds available for doing them. They find ways of making each other most effective and of making maximum use of the knowledge and skills each person brings to the organization.

The *technology* behind each of your organization's new products or services needs to be sufficiently developed far enough that these products or services can be produced and delivered profitably. Much may still need to be learned about the products or services, as well as about the production process, even though production may have already begun.

It is not uncommon for the methods and equipment for mass production to be designed and built while orders are being filled. Furthermore, it often takes longer than planned to get the mass production process up and running. This results in lots of manual construction and/or more steps and rework than is profitable, at least temporarily.

Putting all these in place where they have not existed before is a daunting task. This is why few entrepreneurs make it on their first try.

Common Difficulties

• *Soliciting investment*

Most entrepreneurs are astonished at the amount of time and effort needed to solicit investments and manage investor relations. This is especially true in the case of organizations that develop new-to-the-world offerings in industries that themselves are new, such as biotechnology. Some of these organizations are formed on the basis of a promising process that may take years to perfect, much less produce a profit or something of value, yet huge expenditures may be required during that incubation period.

Few Pioneer start-ups are fully funded. Indeed, most new organizations experience long and painful periods of inadequate financing. This is particularly true if you are not one of the present darlings of investors. You must establish a clear and widespread understanding of your products or services and their potential so that investors are willing to choose your organization from among many possible opportunities. This can be a long and grueling process.

• *Establishing a credible presence in the market*

Establishing credibility often means making lengthy and tedious efforts to influence opinion leaders, providing innumerable free or at-cost demonstration projects, and advertising extensively (and usually expensively) to targeted markets. (This is partly why it is so important to manage time wisely. Many start-up Pioneers have gone under because time ran out before their credibility was established and sufficient demand for their products or services had been built.)

No matter how wonderful your new product or service is, it will almost surely meet fierce resistance at first. Remember that the market has done just fine without your product or service. Furthermore, those who are invested in currently accepted products and services are not likely to easily accept your presence. In fact, they will normally work hard to keep your message from being heard above theirs.

- *Managing the difficulty and intensity of the start-up process*

In some ways, nearly everything done by a Pioneer start-up is difficult. There are no precedents, no paths to follow that assure success, no income to count on from long-term customers that can help the organization weather financial storms, and no detailed, long-term information about sales and expenses to help management know what is really going on. At least at first, everything is being built on educated guesses.

- *Defining the real business*

Establishing the total process that defines the organization is critical to long-term survival. At first, your products and services are the only concrete or definable things to hold on to. Thus, they initially tend to define and determine everything. However, your *real* business may turn out to be the technology that your new product or service represents or the marketing channel that your organization has built or discovered. Figuring this out demands both long-range and strategic thinking—at a time when urgent short-term concerns are constantly eating away at time and resources.

Solutions

- *Define the business as early as possible.*

It is easy to become intoxicated with new products or services. We think they will be so useful and wonderful that customers will be easily won over and that our success will be assured.

The reality is almost always quite different. A set of interlocking forces must come together to create customer demand: availability, visibility, customer need, timing, positioning, luck, and several other forces that are less definable. It often takes considerable experimentation to determine what those forces really are and how to best align your products or services with them. Furthermore, if even one significant part of the puzzle is overlooked or misunderstood, the whole organization can travel down the wrong path. The sooner the puzzle is put together and all assumptions have been checked out with the market, the sooner a clear strategy can be developed and used to focus efforts. Yet this focus is critical; without it, resources get ill-used and wasted.

Some start-ups actually create a position called chief development officer, whose primary responsibilities are to quickly create a viable business definition and to build a strategy for successfully engaging the market.

- *Set your organization's sights on the Jungle or the Kingdom.*

Determine where you expect to take your product or service—into a Jungle market or a Kingdom market—and how it will get the organization there. (Don't expect it to stay in the Frontier for long as 98 percent of all products and services leave the Frontier within eighteen months.) This is a hugely important strategic decision. If it is possible to own and rule the market, it will take very significant effort and a lot of moneya to make that happen. This represents the high-risk side of the venture capitalist's world, where great rewards are possible if a product or service does make it into a Kingdom market.

Most products and services, however, will have to move from the Frontier into a Jungle. If you plan for this, know that you will eventually need to create a very lean process and an organizational culture that can cope with lots of competition.

Your decision on which direction to plan for will be based on a combination of goals, observation, costs, risk tolerance, and as much hard market information as you can acquire.

- *Build a suitable organization for now and for the future.*

The new venture and its culture should, of course, be designed to function in the Frontier but also be thinking about the next iteration of the organization. If the plan is to constantly invent new products, services, or variations and spin them off, provide for this in the design of the organization. Think in terms of building an institution as well as developing product or service lines.

Openly share this vision of the future with all stakeholders. Keep a holistic view in front of everybody. Expect a significant contribution from everyone. Stay lean. Share the rewards.

Consider what is needed to be successful in the next market and, as soon as possible, get your people and processes prepared to be successful in them.

Ensure innovation as a constant, especially if you intend to create a Kingdom. Build fluid structures to allow and encourage sharing rather than competition. Keep bureaucracy to a minimum.

• ***Carefully monitor and manage finances.***

Be realistic about the financing needed to carry out your organization's growth plan. Be assiduous about tracking expenditures and costs of all kinds, from inventory to advertising to payroll. Stay in control of finances at all times even if plenty of funding is available because at some point, it may not be.

• ***Focus and encourage others to do the same.***

As a manager, focus on the two or three things each person in the organization can do to make a difference. Organize the system around those things. Have people come together often to discuss how the process of defining and building the organization is going.

Adaptation Issues

The uncertainties of Frontier markets are great. Managing in this environment sometimes seems like an impossible mission. Most new entrepreneurs operating in Frontier markets find that their organizations eat their lives. This is the stuff from which personal dysfunction is often born or at least nourished. Keeping your life centered and your values intact can be very tough.

Things can be difficult for many of your employees and managers as well, especially if they are not used to Pioneer organizations. The uncertainty is simply too great for many of them. On the other hand, a new breed of person has appeared who wants this kind of life and expects to make a fortune early as a reward for their dedication to a new product, service, or company. In short, for as long as your organization stays in the Frontier, it will be in nonstop transition. Your operating principle will need to be adaptation. There will be no security until you begin operating in a Jungle or a Kingdom.

2. **Moving in from the Jungle with a new product or service that changes the way you do business**

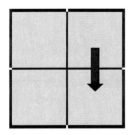

One of your organization's inventions or adaptations is so new and different that it has created a new business and has put you into a new market and/or distribution channel.

You are part of an established organization whose products or services normally compete in very contested markets. The organization relies heavily on innovation to compete with other Hunters. However, its new product or service substantially changes (or will soon change) the way the enterprise does business, moving all or part of it out of a Jungle and into a Frontier.

Key Issues

This situation is both risky and rife with opportunity. On the one hand, innovation is no stranger to your organization. Your people understand the relevant issues and dilemmas very well. On the other, the entire organization has been designed to focus almost entirely on its customers and on the efficiencies needed to operate with ever-shrinking margins. This climate may actually get in the way of your making the most out of your new, potentially dominating product or service.

Furthermore, Hunter organizations often have some difficulty distinguishing between extensions—takeoffs on existing products and services (e.g., audiobooks)—and products and services that are truly new to the world (e.g., e-books). This is because in a Jungle market, almost any improvement or extension causes a product or service to be *marketed* as something supposedly new.

The best way to identify a truly new-to-the-world product or service is that it has the potential to significantly change consumer behavior. Typically (though not necessarily), it also includes or makes use of some new technology.

For example, inkjet printers use a very different technology from both laser and dot matrix printers. It also changed consumer behavior by bringing color printing to the masses. Precisely because Hewlett-Packard's invention was much more than an extension of the laser printer, HP formed a new division to separate its inkjet printers from its laser printers.

In a Hunter organization, designers usually work closely with consumers to figure out exactly what they want and give it to them. But with a new-to-the-world product or service, this process doesn't (and can't) work very well since consumers have little idea what they want yet. A different design process needs to take place, one based in part on intuition and intelligent guesswork.

Furthermore, a Hunter organization's manufacturing systems have been constructed at great cost to build products according to the specifications of customers. In addition, marketing and sales processes have been designed to be congruent with manufacturing. Your new product or service will change some of this. Therefore, unless they are handled properly, the new product or service can become a major disruption to the ongoing business.

Thus it is critical that the new product or service be positioned—and championed—deeply inside the organization so that resistance is lessened and growth is promoted. Leaders in the organization need to inform all stakeholders of how the new product or service fits into its mission. Leaders also need to be clear and forthright about what impact the new product or service will have on employees and on the organization as a whole.

It is equally critical to position the product or service in the market in such a way that it has a chance to grow and thrive. This will likely mean using a new or different set of players for distribution, a different kind of marketing effort, and/or a different long-term market image and presence. The new product or service may also need to be priced and/or even branded differently.

Common Difficulties

- ## *The emergence of internal rivalries*

Even though Hunter organizations are used to dealing constantly with innovation, creating and launching a truly new-to-the-world product or service can create a good deal of friction and resistance.

The new division or unit that emerges will require plenty of time, money, and people to refine the technology, build production capability, create a marketing presence, and develop the necessary infrastructure. As the new venture is built up, more and more resources will typically be siphoned off from other parts of the organization to support the new service, product, or line.

Rivalries can thus begin to develop between people who are under pressure to grow the organization's traditional product and service lines and those who are under the gun to get the new product or service established and out of the red. These are natural and unavoidable rivalries, and they should be expected, planned for, and managed.

- ## *Lack of marketing acceptance and buy-in*

New-to-the-world products and services are not accepted easily by marketing departments that are heavily invested in traditional product and service lines. Truly new products and services may not even show up on their mental radar screens unless management forces the issue. When 3M's marketers were first introduced to Post-it® notes, for example, they thought it was a cute idea, but they resisted any notion that it would change the nature of office communications. It took interventions from outside consultants to simply get a market test, which demonstrated the product's real potential.

- ## *The pressures of a Hunter culture*

No new-to-the-world product or service will be able to withstand the traditional Hunter pressures for immediate high performance, close customer involvement, and continual cost reductions. These can kill the initiative needed to create a product or service that works and is acceptable to customers to develop a mass production process and to create an effective sales and marketing effort. Only a separate Pioneer culture—set up specifically to design, produce, and deliver the new product or service—can provide the appropriate support and initiative.

Solutions

• *Create a new organization.*

It will be tempting to try to keep the new product or service within the ranks of one of your organization's regular lines. *Resist this temptation, however.* If you don't, the organization will quickly become enmeshed in management infighting over resources. Worse still, your front line may refuse to accept the new product or service, let alone give it a higher priority than your traditional product or service lines.

The real question should be how and when to separate the new effort organizationally. Some organizations give it the status of a project, with its own management and personnel, but keep it within the ranks of Hunter management until it is strong enough to function on its own. This can work *if* the project is given a considerable amount of protection from the forces mentioned earlier. There will also need to be strong and enthusiastic leadership in order to secure the resources needed by the project.

Another option is to spin off the effort into a completely new kind of enterprise, a la what GM did with Saturn. This new venture may be completely independent, or it may have some limited alliances with the main Hunter organization. This decision is very much related to how influential—and how helpful or detrimental—the Hunter organization is likely to be. If the long-term plan for the new product or service is to become a Ruler, a distinct separation from the Hunter organization is warranted, but if the future appears to include eventual movement into a Jungle market, it probably would be smarter for the new venture to stay at least minimally connected to the organization's traditional product or service lines.

- ***Provide strategic direction from management around long-term interests.***

At some point, this new effort will begin to look more and more like a start-up. Therefore, the kinds of support needed by start-ups are appropriate here. You will need to bring in the funding, time, and people to get the new product or service into the streets.

However, Hunter managers are notoriously stingy with these resources and want major justification for every significant expenditure. These justifications can take time and energy away from the very activities that are needed to put the new product or service on the map. Certainly, some oversight is needed (and should be provided). But top management needs to be solidly behind the new product or service—financially as well as conceptually. Otherwise, the entire new initiative will have been set up to fail.

The best way to get the necessary buy-in—and the needed commitment of resources—is to develop a clear-cut, long-range plan for weathering the storms of the Frontier and completing the journey to either the Kingdom or the Jungle. Approval of such a plan means that the new effort will not be left high and dry or become subject to attack when some of the inevitable problems of operating in a Frontier arise.

This long-range plan should include set priorities, policies, and practices for operating in both the Frontier now *and* either a Kingdom or a Jungle later on. One example here is pricing. If you have a product or service that is on its way to a Kingdom, prices need to be set with significant margins early on so that the infrastructure and culture needed in a Kingdom market can be afforded. But if the product or service is on its way to the Jungle, then learning how to be successful with tight margins—and preparing the new organization to be decisive, lean, and aggressive—will be very useful.

Many of the early dot-coms failed precisely because they did not make such preparations. As a result of some very successful IPOs, they were initially awash in money and made the mistake of developing very prodigal, opulent cultures. When they faced huge battles in the Internet Jungle, they were ill prepared for it.

- *Generate joint ownership with the marketing department.*

Buy-in from marketers is critical yet often difficult to achieve. One potentially very powerful strategy—and one which can also yield invaluable information—is to include marketers in the design process. Ideally, this cooperation should begin relatively early on and continue indefinitely.

Another useful tool is a series of awareness sessions to be held with marketing staff as soon as the new product or service has been given a go-ahead by top management. In these sessions, introduce marketing people to the new product or service then openly discuss issues such as cash flow, growth timelines and expectations, sales projections, and the effect of the new product or service on current customers and traditional product lines.

Adaptation Issues

- *Managing emotional conflicts and attitudes among employees*

The decision to organizationally separate the new product or service will have an impact on all employees. Some hardcore Hunter types will want to get rid of the new enterprise; others will see the decision to separate the new venture as a lack of trust in them. A variety of other attitudes and emotions—some justified, some not—will also be present.

Management needs to make it abundantly clear to all stakeholders that the purpose of the change is to foster the new product or service *while continuing to grow the traditional ones.* It is vital that management listen to and respect the concerns of everyone who is affected. Some people who remain in the larger Hunter organization will feel left behind. Some going on to the new Pioneer enterprise will be uncomfortable with the displacement and/or the risk.

Management should sponsor open discussions about the present and future changes and the reasons for them. These should not merely be presentations but interactive sessions in which employees are given the chance to express their concerns. Those concerns should of course be taken seriously and addressed to the degree possible. Fears and worries that cannot be effectively addressed should simply be acknowledged.

("Yes, there will be less job security in the new organization. That's a real concern, and it's part of the trade-off for being part of an enterprise that could be very successful and could lead to career advancement and higher pay for you. If you're very concerned about the reduced job security, let Phyllis in HR know and ask her if she can change your assignment.")

Widespread understanding and support are essential to making both the old and the new organization work. Merely expecting people to adjust is insufficient. They *will* adjust eventually, but they will also hold back some of the commitment they could have offered.

There is always more going on under the surface than what people will talk about, and it needs to be addressed if you want people to do their best and stay committed.

- ### *Establishing the right kind of management*

It is crucial to choose the right people to manage the new organization and to choose them in the right way. Leadership positions should *not* be given out as rewards for good work in getting the product or service into the market. (Other kinds of rewards should be given for that.)

Leading a newly formed Pioneer organization into a difficult and ambiguous market environment takes insight, intuition, creativity, and intelligence. Leaders in this new Pioneer organization should also know how to create financial stability throughout the development process. This means being able to get resources and buy-in from top management and to protect the new organization from excessive management scrutiny. Equally important, it means being able to convince people at the top that they need to be patient. In too many organizations, top managers unrealistically expect new products or services to reap huge rewards quickly in order to feed the voracious appetite of Wall Street. This impatience can seriously undermine the discovery process needed to establish a new product, service, or technology. The right person or people at the top of the new Pioneer organization can help top management—a group of superbly skilled Hunters—maintain the proper perspective.

It is also critical that leaders in the new enterprise are able to obtain and maintain the freedom to experiment with the new product or service. They need to be allowed to learn by attempting a variety of approaches and solutions, some of which are bound to fail. In a Hunter organization, such failures are strenuously avoided; in this new Pioneer venture, however, failure should not only be tolerated but considered a necessary step toward success.

- ***Finding the right staff***

It is not enough to have talented, committed people on board in this new organization. They must also be able to function well according to the needs and expectations of a Pioneer organization. In some cases, this may mean hiring people from other Pioneer cultures; in others, it may mean training capable employees from the larger Hunter organization to work in a very different way. Either way, you need to stack the deck with lots of Pioneer employees so that they are a clear dominant influence in the new venture.

In order for people to perform well, managers in the new enterprise need to be very specific about their needs and expectations. When GM spun off Saturn, for example, Saturn's leaders had a specific vision of how its factory was going to be designed, how the organization needed to be structured, and how its people needed to work together to make the venture successful.

It is worth spending the time to create profiles of the kinds of people who will be most successful in this new organization. Then from both the larger Hunter organization and the world at large, seek out talented people who fit these profiles. These will need to be people who can be comfortable with ambiguity, a relative lack of supervision, the possible lack of sufficient resources to do the necessary work, and the vagueness and vagaries of the market.

- ***Creating the right structure for the new organization***

The primary tasks of a Pioneer are to create a product or service, build the capacity to mass-produce it, and secure an entry into the appropriate marketplace. All else, including the design of the new organization, needs to be subordinated to and supportive of these tasks.

The structure of this new organization must allow people the freedom and energy to do jobs that are often ambiguous and difficult. Thus the structure needs to be open and supportive, exactly the opposite of the structure of a Warrior organization. Some tasks will be done by everyone as a team; others will require just a few people or only one. The work groups and relationships will change as the work changes. Some individuals will rise to the forefront of the group at times; others will come to the fore at other times. The only accountability will be the overall progress on the primary tasks and the helpfulness of the support activities. Since the primary tasks will take all the talent present in the group, every effort needs to be made to get the most out of each person. All this needs to be encouraged and supported by management.

There are some similarities here to what goes on in Hunter organizations, where teams are often the norm. However, what is different is the fluidity of the structure. In a Pioneer organization, work arrangements change like the weather, from teams to partners to individual initiative then back again, depending on the task.

- *Managing the politics of innovation*

When new products and services are developed, they tend to gather sponsors and *owners*. Each owner would like their own particular products and services to succeed, sometimes instead of other new products or services and, occasionally, instead of the larger organization's traditional product or service lines. These owners become active in a process of political influence that creates winners and losers within the organization. This is often entirely unrelated to whether any product, service, or line is better for the organization than another.

Three of the ongoing tasks of leaders in this new Pioneer organization are (1) discovering who the various sponsors and owners are, (2) determining what will help them to provide the most constructive support for the organization, and (3) engaging them sufficiently and in the right way so that they provide that support. Ideally, these sponsors should be coaxed into championing the new venture; if that is not possible, then they at least need to accept its presence and its validity. If leaders fail to attend to this task, a surprisingly large amount of effort and focus can easily be wasted in infighting and political maneuvering.

3. **A Battleground organization puts resources into new-to-the-world products or services**

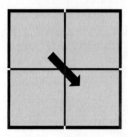

After your organization's regular product or service lines have become commoditized, it develops a new product or service for which there is no already-developed market.

Warriors and Pioneers are diametrically opposed. Warriors think in terms of similarity rather than innovation and usually oppose (sometimes with a vengeance) any significant changes to their products and services. This is necessary when dealing with extremely high volumes and low margins. In contrast, differences are not only important to Pioneers but highly valued by them.

Rulers and Hunters normally have at least some need for innovation. Warriors, however, generally do not, beyond finding ways to improve the manufacturing and distribution of their traditional products and services. Thus, changing from a Warrior to a Pioneer organization is the most difficult of the twelve types of changes an organization can make. It is also the least common.

Though rare, it is possible for a new product, service, or process to be born in a Warrior organization, particularly if the Warrior has been involved in a merger or acquisition. When it does happen, most often the wisest response is to sell the discovery to another, more Pioneering organization.

But sometimes a Warrior may choose to develop the new product or service itself. Let's look at the factors that need to be considered and addressed.

Key Issues

To move from a large commodity-producing entity to an organization trying to find a market for a largely unknown product or service is a huge structural and cultural change. Why would management get involved in this kind of business? Whatever the answer to this question—and there are a few valid ones—that answer needs to be communicated extremely clearly and visibly to everyone affected. This message needs to be repeated and emphasized over and over because Warriors' natural tendencies are antithetical to what is needed in the new start-up.

Common Difficulties

Warrior cultures are designed to accelerate, improve, and streamline the production of a known entity. Their focus is on volume, speed, and quality in the production process. All their innovation centers on these activities, not on creating new products or services.

A Pioneer project thus has to be staffed entirely from the outside in order to succeed. *Management must understand from the start that this is an absolute requirement.*

One of the Pioneer's biggest concerns is having enough resources to develop a product or service that is at least partly unknown and untested in the market. Such an investment is foreign to Warrior management. This means that the new Pioneer will need to have a reliable funding source outside the avenues normally used in the larger organization.

Solutions

In general, I recommend against even attempting this kind of change. If your organization is considering such a transformation, however, keep the following points in mind:

- From the start, completely separate the new Pioneer enterprise from any part of the Warrior organization. The two should have their own distinct missions, people, and cultures. If possible, they should also be in separate physical locations.

- Make sure the Warrior organization exerts no influence whatsoever on the Pioneer. It may provide financial support, however, provided that support comes with very few or no strings attached.
- Every leader in the new Pioneer enterprise—and if possible, many of its employees—should have significant experience working in Pioneer organizations. Top leadership must also have experience in designing and managing Pioneer ventures.
- The new Pioneer enterprise must be driven by a very clear new product / new service vision rather than a vision to someday be a part of the Warrior organization. The future of the business should be in either a Jungle or Kingdom, *never* in a Battleground.

Adaptation Issues

The guiding philosophy of a Warrior organization is to create order and sameness in production and to do things ever faster and more efficiently. The new Pioneer venture, however, should favor newness and innovation over speed, and it will very likely disdain order.

What makes a Warrior organization profitable is the presence of systems that work the same all the time. In contrast, the new Pioneer enterprise will have little that is formal and standardized; its systems will be imperfect and fluid, changing all the time. Much of what is done is being done for the first time. It is a learning environment, finding out about the product or service, the market, the distribution channel, and so on.

Making a transition from order to creative chaos and from inflexible systems to hardly any system at all is next to impossible. This is why the new Pioneer venture must be kept entirely separate from its Warrior owner.

4. **From the Kingdom, when your continuing effort to produce new products or services creates a new industry, product or service category, or marketing channel**

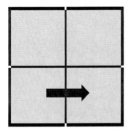

The innovation needed to maintain your organization's dominance in the market is so successful that—perhaps unexpectedly—you are poised to enter the Frontier.

The challenge is to transform this Frontier market into part of your organization's Kingdom before anyone else has a chance to create significant competition. Leaders of every Ruler organizations dream of this happening, yet when it does, it typically creates great (though temporary) stresses and disruptions. If these can be weathered and worked through—and usually they can be—then your Ruler organization has an excellent chance of dramatically expanding its empire.

Ruler organizations have the resources to follow the development trail wherever it goes and to adequately support it with people, marketing, technology, or whatever is needed to make the new product or service a success. Most Ruler organizations spend large amounts of money attempting to come up with these breakthroughs because they know that scoring on even one will provide excellent margins and income for many years. These margins, in turn, can support further R&D efforts (as well as the other expensive attributes of a Ruler culture). However, such breakthroughs are rare and may elude an organization for many years, forcing it to rely on its standard product and service lines and extensions thereof.

As any R&D person can tell you, the discovery process is often quite unpredictable and chancy. Furthermore, once a new product or service has been invented, it may not be recognized as a breakthrough, at least at first. This can be true not only among potential customers but *within the organization itself*. Leaders in Ruler organizations are not always willing to fully accept what an innovation or new technology can lead to or where it can take the organization. In part, this is because of the big internal disruption they know it will cause; in part, it is because other product or service lines—and other agendas—are often more demanding of their attention.

Key Issues

- ### *Managing the opportunity*

Breakthrough opportunities do not necessarily present themselves at ideal times. It may not be easy (or politically viable) to take time, money, and people away from other priorities so that the new product or service gets everything it needs to succeed. While Rulers have the resources to provide such support, they are usually fully deployed in other pursuits. Management therefore needs to create an environment within the organization for the new product or service to succeed. Usually, the required technology, production, and marketing resources already exist; the trick is capturing them away from other priorities and, as much as possible, adding to them. It also means helping everyone in the organization to see the potential of the new idea.

When a Ruler's potentially breakthrough product or service fails, it is typically because management has been able to sell the idea within the organization and capture the right amount of support. For example, several companies could not see the potential of plain paper copiers when the concept was presented by its inventor. As a result, they lost a huge opportunity that Xerox capitalized on.

- ### *Moving quickly enough*

As a result of competition, evolving technology, and greatly improved processes, new products and services can now be brought to market much more quickly than in the past. Yet Ruler management is not used to moving fast. Thus managers need to find ways to accelerate the pace of development so that the new product or service can keep pace with life in a Frontier. This is not easy since the prevailing notion among inventors is that much of what happens is serendipity and is not subject to planning or programming.

- *Allocating sufficient resources*

Ruler organizations do not have to beg investors for resources. This saves a great deal of time and effort and gives Rulers a distinct advantage when they enter the Frontier. However, if managers must spend too much time begging for resources internally or constructing elaborate business cases or plans, they may lose some or all this advantage. If management in your own organization cannot or will not provide the necessary resources in a timely fashion, you are probably better off not attempting to enter the Frontier. Instead, sell off the new product, service, or process to another organization.

- *Managing the vulnerability of the new product or service*

New products, services, processes, and concepts are fragile and vulnerable. They can easily be dismissed or viewed as distractions from the business at hand. They need to be protected from too much management scrutiny, especially early in the development process, as well as from other parts of the organization that may view the new venture as competition or even a threat.

Common Difficulties

- *Pressure to produce profits too soon*

In a Ruler organization, it is easy to forget that there is always a development curve for new products and services and that living through the beginning of the curve is always costly and painful. There will thus be pressure to produce unrealistically strong results unrealistically fast.

This pressure needs to be managed, not disregarded. The struggle between forces that insist on additional time and patience (e.g., R&D) and those that fight to shorten the development stage (e.g., marketing) is natural and, to a point, even beneficial. Both are legitimate forces that must be balanced, mediated, and if possible, synthesized.

- ### *Resistance from the bureaucracy*

A Ruler organization's bureaucracy is necessary to support its aggressive market control. Within this bureaucracy are leaders with agendas of all kinds that they would like to push forward. While a Ruler culture normally encourages this, it is not particularly conducive to the development of a new product or service. Some leaders who are trying to build their own internal fiefdoms will try to make it quite difficult for the new enterprise to secure resources. They will do this indirectly by withholding help, prioritizing other products and services, or distracting the attention of management. Furthermore, some Ruler managers may actually support and encourage this behavior on the theory that new ideas need to prove themselves by surviving the bureaucratic gauntlet of resistance, subversion, and indifference.

- ### *Lack of focus*

Ruler organizations need to resist the temptation to develop too many new products or services at once based on the concept that if only one out of twenty (or thirty or one hundred) succeeds, the margins will more than justify the effort. (I once counted twenty-six new products being developed simultaneously *in a single division* of a manufacturing company.) The dangers here are twofold: first, that no one development effort is given the resources it needs to succeed and, second, that some of those efforts may not support the strategic direction of the organization.

Another unfortunate but common result is that the most promising ideas get pushed aside in favor of the pet projects championed by managers who are better at pushing their agendas and getting their way.

- ### *Inappropriate leadership*

The people who invent and develop new products, services, processes, and technologies are often made the early leaders of these new ventures. This is not usually a wise idea, however. Techies are not necessarily good business people, and seldom are they good managers. Indeed, many would rather *not* have to manage a project, especially the people issues, yet how many of them are going to turn down an opportunity to spearhead a new venture? Even if they want to, few will dare because their loyalty and commitment will be questioned forever after.

Furthermore, technical people are not always the most psychologically stable. I'm not suggesting that they have serious character flaws but that the long hours and concentration needed to make something out of nothing can take an enormous emotional toll. There are notable exceptions to this, of course, but in my experience, they are few.

Yet we somehow expect these people, who are typically more interested in ideas and things than in relationships, to secure adequate funding from management, create or determine the right distribution channel, roll out a product or service that is not yet well understood, handle all the people issues perfectly, and develop all the right relationships to make each of these things happen.

Solutions

- ***Honor and support entrepreneurs.***

You will need to create a culture that honors, supports, respects, and thrives on innovators and entrepreneurs. This is particularly important for Rulers since this helps them stay ahead of the competition and maintain control of the market.

It will take consistent and powerful leadership to establish the necessary cooperative behaviors and attitudes. Many cross-organizational projects, associations, standing committees, reward traditions, and management-development activities will be needed to supplant the natural political process that permeates a Ruler system.

I once facilitated a meeting that included entrepreneurs from a Pioneer division of a Fortune 500 company as well as leaders from a Ruler organization who wanted to learn more about developing new products. The Pioneer types explained that in their division, everyone was expected to share their knowledge, discoveries, equipment, and other resources with anyone else who was developing a product and needed help. Furthermore, no project numbers were ever asked for or provided; help was given without any expectations or any need for accountings or justification. This arrangement totally astounded the Ruler managers.

- *Protect the new product or service.*

Although there will be serious competition for resources within a Ruler organization, this struggle is propelled more by politics than by scarcity. There may well be sufficient resources to do everything the organization wants to do, but each leader nevertheless does all they can to capture the biggest possible slice of the pie. This is normal in a Ruler organization; in a culture based largely on protectionism, each manager is simply protecting their unit, division, or department from being seen as less important than some new upstart.

This means, oddly enough, that *it is crucial to keep top management in the dark about a concept for a new-to-the-world product or service during its early phases of development.* Once it does get presented to leaders, the new venture should be separated as soon as possible from the rest of the organization so that it is not subject to as many political pressures.

The new enterprise might, for example, become a separate project with its own project manager. This person should report to someone in top management (ideally, a vice president or someone even higher up) who has a keen respect for the strategic potential of the enterprise.

At the earliest possible time, the new enterprise needs to be positioned internally as a legitimate product or service of the Ruler organization. This should be done even if—indeed, especially if—the venture is a long way from producing revenue and becoming self-sustaining. This enables top management to remove many of the political concerns that may come from other units or divisions.

- *Proactively develop entrepreneurial management.*

Entrepreneurs within a large organization are not, at heart, very different from those who are just starting their own businesses. They typically have the same idiosyncrasies—e.g., a passion for innovation, a need for attention, and personal issues around control. Usually, they are not very good at—and are often naive about—corporate politics. Thus they can end up being vulnerable to the maneuvers of managers with more political savvy.

It is very difficult to develop entrepreneurial skills and attitudes among the ranks of typical Ruler managers. It makes far more sense, then, to locate the entrepreneurial types—people who are comfortable working outside the organization's standard frames of reference—within the organization but outside of management, and proactively train them in management skills and techniques.

Finding these people and nourishing them is crucial to developing and marketing new-to-the-world products and services. Once trained, they will be able to set up an iconoclastic new enterprise and develop it into a Ruler of its own Kingdom market—at which point the larger organization will be able to assimilate it easily.

This means several things. First, you need to be finding and developing these people regardless of whether your organization has (or is even working on) any new-to-the-world products or services. Second, this selection and training process can't be haphazard or casual. You need to create a very deliberate process to find these folks within the present ranks. Third, never lose sight of the fact that these people are willing to go up against the accepted norms and stretch your organization's ability to allow for diversity in thinking. They will begin doing this long before there is a need for them to do so or even a new Pioneer enterprise for them to do it in. This means protecting them from any potential wrath or punishment from the people in the Ruler organization whom they may challenge. It also means being very clear with them about the difference between what the organization needs from them right now and what a new Pioneer enterprise may require from them in the future.

In a Ruler organization, entrepreneurs are both vulnerable and difficult to live with. For this reason, it is important to have places for them to go, coaching from top managers, and ways for them to feel that they are valued by the organization. Reward them as best you can without incurring too much political fallout from other quarters. Encourage them to meet with, support, and coach each other. Help them to set up support mechanisms that will be useful to other people like them.

- ***Make resources reasonably available.***

The struggle to obtain resources can make life very difficult for entrepreneurs. If this process takes on too much political baggage, they will lose much of their commitment and motivation and may even leave the organization. Furthermore, if a Pioneer leader is too busy trying to find resources for their project, the necessary work will not get done, deadlines will not be met, everything will slow down, and some other organization will gain the all-important first foothold in the market. It is critical, therefore, that management prioritize projects and give the leader of the new enterprise the resources they need.

- ***Allocate development funds strategically.***

All of the above underscores how important it is to let go of many of the traditional attitudes about developing new products and services. In the twenty-first century, new offerings simply will not make it to market fast enough if management has a laissez-faire attitude about them or does not make a sufficient commitment to the necessary technologies.

Furthermore, in the twenty-first century, even Ruler organizations cannot afford to support a wide range of eclectic development efforts, especially if some are funded not for sound business reasons but because they are the pet projects of managers who have created politically protected environments. Top management must weigh each project against the organization's strategic direction, then they need to take a deep breath and say no to anything that doesn't support that direction.

The risk of not doing this is that your organization could develop some wonderful and lucrative new-to-the-world products and services yet still spend more on development than those new offerings bring in. For many Rulers, this is a very difficult lesson to learn.

Adaptation Issues

- ***Helping managers to understand and accept the Pioneer enterprise***

In developing new-to-the-world products or services, Ruler organizations need to use a repeatable pattern or process. This avoids having to learn the same lessons over again. This pattern or process should include a mini training course for managers, both entrepreneurs in the new venture and traditional Ruler managers in the larger organization. The course should coach them on the following:

- What kinds of people are needed to manage each phase of the new venture's development
- What kind of structure is needed in the new venture
- How Pioneers can survive among Rulers
- The transition to a Ruler organization that will occur should the new venture ultimately control the market

- ***Planning for the transition to a Ruler***

The goal of the new venture is to conquer the new market and bring it into the Ruler's fold. *This needs to be prominently and repeatedly communicated to everyone in the organization throughout the development phase.* People need to understand from the start that the Pioneer culture will not last indefinitely.

Most of all, the leader of the new Pioneer venture needs to understand that if they succeed, the unit or division will be handed over to a Ruler manager, who will then establish a Ruler culture. They should also, of course, be assured that when this time comes, they will be well rewarded and given another appropriate assignment.

Actually, managers in *any* Pioneer organization would do well to frequently remind employees that their enterprise will probably move out of the Frontier fairly quickly, normally within a year or two and, almost certainly, within three or four. While it is possible for an organization to remain a Hunter, a Warrior, or a Ruler for decades, the dynamics of markets make it very rare for an organization to enter a Frontier and stay there for any length of time.

One final word on Pioneer organizations in general: working in one is like living in a frying pan. Managing stress, both personally and organizationally, is essential. Regardless of what direction you've entered the Frontier from, create some mechanisms to keep things from boiling over. Deliberately build some humor and other stress-reducing activities (meditation and yoga classes, exercise opportunities, goofy contests, etc.) into your culture. Encourage people to lighten up when they can and make sure that you do the same.

PART FIVE

Leading the Twenty-First Century Organization

CHAPTER THIRTEEN

Managing the Change

This chapter will give you a wide-angle view of the entire process described in the previous chapters. In addition, it will show you how to derive the most benefit from all the tools, processes, and concepts presented thus far.

Over time, your goal should be to embed these tools, processes, and concepts deeper and deeper in your organization so that they become normal parts of assessment, planning, strategy, and organizational life in general. However, they should *not* replace the strategic planning activities you are already using to guide your organization. Rather, they should be used in conjunction with them, to give them greater clarity, strength, and direction.

Each division, unit, and department in an organization typically has its own subculture, characteristics, and norms and, as a result, its own ideal management style. Thus, in a single organization, it may sometimes, for example, make sense to look at R&D as a Pioneer department, at marketing as a Hunter department, and at manufacturing as a Warrior department even though the overall organization may be a Ruler doing business in a Kingdom market. Management needs to understand how to address not only the Ruler issues of the whole organization but also the Pioneer issues of R&D, the Hunter issues of marketing, and the Warrior issues of manufacturing. Furthermore, the people running these departments need to understand how the different subcultures work and can best interact.

Where Archetypes and Strategy Meet

Any strategic planning in your organization should begin with a current assessment of its environment and culture—that is, with an up-to-date organization/market profile. Indeed, the use of this profile necessarily pushes the issue of organizational culture to the forefront of strategic planning. (This profile can also be used to help shape more specific strategies on investment, acquisitions, new product development, and restructuring.)

The organization-market profile has been used successfully as a strategic planning tool by many organizations throughout the world, including 3M, KPMG Europe, Merck Mid-Europe, Snap-On Tools, and RTW Insurance, and especially in the small- to medium-size companies. The process is especially helpful in family-owned businesses that need ways to get everyone on board with a new direction.

Family businesses often encounter critical times when it seems like a new direction is needed or it doesn't seem possible to move to another level of growth. Getting an understanding from all the stakeholders is not easy, and the PerfectBizMatch process can be very useful in providing a landscape that all can understand and strategize around.

Let's look at how the profile can be used in strategic planning by considering one such real-life example: a midsize enterprise that had manufactured specialty tools for automobiles for some thirty years but which seemed to be stagnating. We will call it the Specialty Tool Company (STC).

STC had all its top managers take the assessment and create their own organization/market profiles. It then held a retreat for these managers to help them better understand the company's markets and make any necessary adaptations. In this retreat, leaders realized that they needed to separate their product lines into two categories: (1) hard tools, which were commodities being sold in a Battleground market, and (2) electronic handheld devices, which were high-tech, customizable products being sold in a Jungle market. As the retreat progressed, they discovered that the issues around serving customers were very different for these two groups of products. As a result, STC changed its company structure, creating two different cultures—a Warrior culture and a Hunter culture—that operate side by side.

Your own organization/market profile can be used to help you and your colleagues reach consensus on major business line and organizational issues. Ultimately, you will make some judgments about the following:

- What market environments you will compete in
- What products and/or services you will offer
- How you will engage the competition
- How you will alter the organization's culture
- How you will alter the organization's operating style

You can also use the questions from the Archetype Assessment as valuable discussion tools. Although the assessment is intended to be taken individually by key people in an organization, its questions (and people's answers) can also be presented to groups to provoke thoughtful analysis, debate, and deliberation. Such discussions can, in turn, create very high levels of creativity, problem solving, buy-in, and commitment.

Using Archetypes in Strategic Planning

I have developed a six-step model for making best use of the Archetype Assessment in strategic planning and decision making. To use this model most effectively, the entire process should be driven by the leader of the organization and championed by all members of the leadership team.

If the organization doing the planning is an individual department—say, human resources—then the people to involve would probably be limited to a handful of department managers, some key HR employees, and the vice president of operations, but if the entire division is creating a strategic plan, then all top managers from the division, all department leaders, and key people from the larger organization should be included. In the case of division-wide and organization-wide planning, each relevant unit needs to go through a similar process so that there is consistency in the results.

Here are some suggested steps in this process:

1. Have all the relevant managers complete the Archetype Assessment individually. Collect and tabulate their answers to each question. Also collect all their organization/environment profiles. (Individual answers, scores, and profiles should, of course, be kept confidential or, preferably, anonymous.)

2. Hold an initial retreat, forum, or discussion based on the assessment. Top management should lead this event.

   Begin the event by displaying the range of responses to each question, then let managers ask questions about each others' responses. These questions will help determine who else needs to be involved in the decision-making process and who else can provide helpful insight or information. For example, frontline people and others close to customers can often provide down-to-earth knowledge that will keep everyone focused and realistic.

   One goal of these discussions is to develop a common understanding of the questions themselves as a step toward creating an agreed-upon view of the present market and the organization's culture and structure.

   Toward the middle or the end of this session, participants should create a common organization-market profile that includes or acknowledges the full range of responses. This should be done through discussion, disagreement, debate, and an eventual consensus; the common profile should *not* be a statistical composite.

3. Distribute copies of this common profile and the range of responses to each assessment question to all relevant parties for their review.

4. Hold a second retreat, forum, or discussion. This should include all the people from the first session as well as anyone else who was identified as necessary or helpful to the strategic planning process.

   Anyone who will be central to the implementation of the strategic plan should also be involved in planning. Partly, this is an issue of buy-in and commitment; partly, it is one of efficiency. The addition of more people to the process means that it may take longer to create an acceptable plan, but the implementation process will be much faster and easier as a result.

The goal of this retreat should be to establish a consensus on the future direction of the organization in terms of its markets, its structure, and its culture. However, don't rush to reach any quick decisions about what markets to compete in and what type of organization to become. Allow a consensus to evolve rather than attempt to construct a hurried, mechanistic solution.

In many organizations, what top management sees—both in the marketplace and in the organization itself—may be at odds with what is seen by people further down in the organization, where the needs and expectations of customers are more obvious. *Neither group has a full 360-degree view,* and some departments' views will be skewed by the type of functions they perform. For this reason, it is critical to collect and consider all these views and then reach consensus at the top on each key issue.

Lastly, it is not unusual for people—even those who work closely together—to express very diverse views. Indeed, in any group of ten managers, four to eight are going to disagree on some key issues. This is an unavoidable fact of organizational life. This is yet another reason why the strategic planning process should involve whomever will be needed to make change happen.

5. Top management should create a draft document that spells out the details of its strategic vision and how it will be implemented. This tentative strategic plan should then be distributed to everyone who took the Archetype Assessment, along with a request for their review and comments. Each should also be asked what they feel it would take to successfully implement the suggested changes.

6. Using this feedback, top management should design, implement, and fervently promote a final strategic plan.

Getting the Best Results

As you work through the steps of the strategic planning process, keep the following considerations and guidelines in mind:

- *Carefully determine and communicate the boundaries of the organization to be assessed.*

Clearly specify what each participant should consider "the organization." Should they think only of their own department? their division? the entire organization?

- *Determine, clarify, and communicate the goals of the assessment.*

Make it clear to everyone which issues are of greatest concern to management. Are there specific problems the organization hopes to address? In what areas does it strive to be more proactive? Does it seek to better understand what its primary market may be like two years from now?

For ethical reasons, you will also need to be explicit about how the results of the assessment will be used.

- *Prepare participants for taking the assessment.*

In order for everyone to participate with open minds and without fear, they must know from top management exactly what the process is, what it hopes to get out of it, what follow-up management is willing to guarantee, and how each part of the process contributes to the overall effort. They must also know and be able to trust that all their answers and scores will be kept confidential or anonymous.

- *Assure all participants that there are no wrong answers.*

Each person's view influences how they work and what they expect to happen in the organization. By definition, then, people's expectations are powerful and real (though not necessarily accurate) and need to be respected.

- *Help people to fill out the assessment honestly, completely, and thoughtfully.*

People need privacy, adequate time, a reasonably comfortable space, and an open atmosphere so that they do not feel they must answer according to some specific view. This is a critical part of the process, yet it is often overlooked or seen as unimportant.

- *Emphasize consensus in creating a common profile.*

The common profile should reflect the opinion of the group as a whole, including any dissenting views. However, creating this profile should *not* be a voting exercise. It should be a learning and sharing activity without undue influence from any one person.

- *Tabulate all scores from all relevant units then distribute them to everyone in those units; also give these people the composite scores and common profile from the strategic planning sessions.*

The scores in one unit or department may differ significantly from those in another, so people need to see both the larger picture and the differing views of their colleagues.

In addition, if a small but significant number of people in several departments share the same viewpoint or concern, this process increases their likelihood of being listened to and taken seriously.

- *Develop clear, detailed recommendations.*

Top management needs to make the results of this process part of the organization's strategic plan. These results should take the form of recommendations that specify what needs to happen to the organization's market position, what strategies will be undertaken to get to that position, and what will happen to specific projects, products, or services.

In addition, a vision needs to be developed and articulated that shows what needs to happen within the organization in order for the strategic plan to succeed. This should include specific changes in organizational structure, practices, and culture—all explained in sufficient detail to show how everyone will be affected, how they will fit in to the modified organization, and how they will be able to contribute to the new goals.

Lastly, top management needs to be clear and detailed about the changes that will be made in the system at the top and how people at lower levels will form their own processes to implement changes according to the plan.

• ***Show that you're serious; lead from the top.***

Everything suggested in this section needs to be driven by a central team and coached by a top manager. Furthermore, the person at the top of the organization needs to champion the whole process in accordance with the best practices for managing change.

Guidelines for Large-Scale Change

Significant change does not come easily. Most people, even those who believe things need to change, typically think that what needs to change is outside of their own area.

Ultimately, all changes need to be personalized. By this I mean that each person's responsibilities and activities need to be examined for their effectiveness and speed, held up to a new standard, and adjusted or redesigned as needed. No one likes this, and most people will fear and resist it. Even those who are most vocal about the need for change may be fearful inside and may be unprepared for what needs to happen, yet all these people will need to learn a new way of doing familiar things.

If your score on the organization/market profile is 3–5, the change envisioned should include giving people the time to understand, accept, and (when appropriate) design the changes they will undergo. This allows change to proceed at a relatively natural pace and enables the whole change process to be somewhat organic. It will also keep you from losing too many talented managers and employees. New structures will get put into place, and processes will get examined and redesigned, all at a moderate and manageable pace.

However, if your score is 6 or more, time is a major factor. If you do not act quickly, your situation will probably deteriorate at an ever-faster pace. Thus, the whole system needs to be redesigned from the top down—and fast. New management must be put in place swiftly. In turn, these people need to quickly design and implement very new and different ways of doing things. Furthermore, all this needs to be done incisively and with confidence. It will seem messy because so many people will be adversely affected, but it is absolutely essential to the organization's survival.

The immediate goal is to stop the bleeding. The most serious problems need to be taken on first. This typically means removing people, closing down departments, starting new operations, creating and using new scorecards, and demanding new levels of participation.

This process should be driven by the top manager, who should be deeply involved in all aspects of the change. This person needs to have a clear vision, one that they share with other people at the top, of what the organization will look like when the transformation is complete.

These changes will be devastating to most of the people involved. Some will not be able to let go of the inevitable inconsistencies in the treatment of employees, which they will perceive as unfairness. These people will need to leave the organization one way or the other.

After all the changes that can be made from the top have been made and the critical processes redesigned and put in place, the entire organization needs to go through a formal rebuilding of its culture. It is important to identify all the people who will play important roles in the new system and to include all of them in this process. Furthermore, this process needs to be facilitated by a trusted person from outside the system because it will be hard to trust anyone within the organization who has gone through all the trauma.

Thus far in this chapter, I have spoken of the Archetype Assessment and the organization-market profile as tools for creating an initial alignment between your organization and its markets. Once this has been accomplished, however, the Archetype Assessment can also be used to stave off any future need for major restructuring. If you use the assessment and profile appropriately and well, regularly assessing both your organization and its markets, you will keep on top of developments, avoid having to undergo dramatic changes, and stay poised to compete, succeed, and thrive.

CHAPTER FOURTEEN

Implications for Business Leaders

In organizational life, some of what initially appears to be chaotic and arbitrary can, in fact, be understood and predicted, but this can only be done by taking a long view, observing how patterns develop over time, and examining the interrelationship of events.

Some common patterns exist in the way organizations respond to the market environments they encounter. Once we identify and understand these patterns, we can begin to predict and understand the systems at work behind them and, thus, deal with them more effectively.

In any well-managed organization, managers at all levels more or less continuously monitor the interplay between the organization and its markets. Because both behave in some predictable and understandable ways, these managers can then use their observations to plan effectively.

Actually, managers aren't the only people who should do this. In the pages that follow, we'll look at many of the different people who can benefit from the business-matching process and examine how each one uses it to improve their performance.

This is not an exhaustive list, nor will I present all the ways in which each player can use the process effectively. Rather, the descriptions and discussions in this chapter are meant to stimulate your thinking and deepen your understanding.

CEOs

The CEO of an organization is responsible for its growth and development. They lead the strategic planning process and make sure that the resources needed to carry out any strategy are provided.

A CEO must also lead any effort to acquire or merge with another organization in order to accelerate the rate of growth, overtake competition, add capacity or capabilities, and/or consolidate the industry.

However, joining with another organization inevitably has many business-matching implications. The two organizations usually have significantly different histories and experiences even if they have both competed in the same market in similar ways—e.g., even if they are both Hunters who have used similar strategies to succeed in a Jungle market. The cultures and practices of any two organizations can be vastly different. This is especially true if the two organizations do not share the same archetype—e.g., if one is a Ruler and the other a Pioneer. All this can stall or seriously impede the assimilation process. Part of a CEO's job is to make sure that people in both organizations acknowledge and understand their differences. Another part is to lead the development of clear, effective strategies for integrating the new organization. These strategies should be designed so that they can be implemented by all managers in all units.

To support the business-matching process, CEOs need to do the following:

1. *Continuously monitor and assess both the market and the competition,* especially when major changes or events occur.
2. *Establish benchmarks that will show when a product or service has crossed the line into a new market environment.*
3. *Lead the development of a long-term strategy for continuously repositioning products and services in the market* so that the organization can quickly mobilize in response to market changes. Mapping the evolution of each product or service—i.e., regularly plotting its ever-changing position on the archetype grid—should be a part of all strategic planning.
4. *Lead all dialogue and decision making involving the business-matching process.*
5. *Fully understand the dynamics of every business match*—i.e., every decision to compete in a particular market with a specific product or service.
6. *Develop a commitment among leadership to maintain as close a match between the organization and its markets as possible.*

7. *Clearly communicate the organization's long-term strategy to everyone in the organization.* CEOs should use business-matching language to help people understand the strategic moves and adaptations that will be needed for success.

8. *With leaders from HR, establish a monitoring and matching process that continually adapts the organization's personnel to market developments.* Adaptations might include training and development, hiring and/or firing, redesigning jobs, creating (and sometimes disbanding) teams, or reorganizing departments or reporting arrangements.

9. *Use business-matching concepts in dealing with vendors, competitors, and customers as well as in arranging acquisitions or mergers.* CEOs should also encourage everyone in the organization to do the same.

As they perform these tasks, CEOs need to avoid or address these pitfalls:

- *Terminal uniqueness*

The biggest (and most destructive) trap for a CEO is believing that no other organization is truly like their own and, therefore, no system can truly predict what will (or might) happen. This attitude gives the CEO *carte blanche* to run their organization by the seat of their pants based on what they alone are able to see. CEOs who succumb to this temptation thus lead with little or no guidance other than their own experience. This was the cause of death of many of the dot-coms that went under in early 2001. Founders are particularly prey to this syndrome.

- *Failing to clearly define acceptable levels of profit and loss*

CEOs need to identify clear indicators of when a cultural change needs to begin. Without such indicators, decisions on things like belt-tightening, reorganizing, or additional investment in new products may be made capriciously and, often, either prematurely or too late.

- ***An unwillingness to see the cultural and organizational implications of a decision***

Every decision and action has consequences. Some of these will be unintentional and unanticipated; nevertheless, failing to consider the ones that *can* be anticipated is sheer folly. For example, no CEO who initiates significant cost cutting should pretend that their workforce's productivity and effectiveness won't diminish as a result.

- ***Management hubris***

One common example of this is deciding that the organization is going to have the kind of culture that top managers are most comfortable with rather than the type needed to succeed in the chosen market.

- ***An unwillingness to recognize and accept that an organization they do business with operates as a different archetype***

This might be a competitor, a customer, a vendor, or a potential acquisition or merger candidate.

Middle Managers

Middle managers see to it that the work required by a business strategy actually gets done. They establish the mechanisms that integrate resources and develop the processes that do the work effectively and efficiently. They are also in charge of ensuring that people and resources get mobilized in the right ways at the right times.

Without a clear understanding of the business-matching process, however, middle managers may not have the wide-angle view they need to guide all these activities as wisely as possible. Indeed, many business strategies have failed because middle managers did not mobilize the right people and resources quickly enough.

Middle managers will find the business-matching process especially useful in this regard because each type of organization requires its own method of mobilizing resources and implementing strategy. For example, if a middle manager has a semibureaucratic vision of a layered sales force—as would be appropriate for a Ruler organization serving a Kingdom market—and attempts to use that vision for organizing a sales effort in a Jungle environment, the whole sales department will quickly run into big trouble. It will soon become apparent that there are not enough people and that coordinating all the tasks will be agonizingly complex. Likewise, if an operations manager from a Jungle organization tries to set up highly flexible operations in a Warrior business—where the uniformity of processes and products is crucial— the whole enterprise can begin to come apart.

It is critical that top and middle management share a common map and language about the market, the position of their organization in that market, and the strategic direction in which the organization is trying to move. The basic tools and concepts of this book can be very useful in this regard. In addition, the process described in chapter 11 can help middle managers make wise decisions about organizational and process management.

To support the business-matching process, middle managers need to do the following:

1. Completely align with top management about
   - what archetype their organization represents and where it is currently positioned on the archetype grid,
   - what type of market it operates in (and/or seeks to operate in),
   - where each of its product or services is currently positioned on the archetype grid, and
   - what kind of organization and culture are needed to succeed both in the short and long run.
2. Monitor the market continuously and adjust and redesign processes as needed so they are in sync with conditions.
3. Consider each of the other units, functions, departments, and organizations that they need to deal or work with regularly. Middle managers need to identify which ones represent which archetypes; as necessary, they should examine and address potential conflicts in dealing with these entities.
4. *Use business-matching language to help people in the organization understand the operational moves and adaptations that will be necessary for success.* Specific benchmarks and measurements

(e.g., sales levels that would indicate a shift into a new market environment) should be included whenever possible.

As they perform these tasks, middle managers need to avoid or address these pitfalls:

- **Potential conflicts between unit goals and market demands**

Middle managers tend to focus on what needs adjustment or improvement at their level. Thus they often become convinced that the operation needs a change that, to them, seems self-evident. However, it is not uncommon for these *obvious* adjustments or improvements to be exactly the opposite of what is actually needed to succeed under current market conditions.

- **Continuous change but limited current information**

Organizations and their markets are in constant flux. Middle managers know this all too well. Thus, if they lack up-to-date information on the market, they will naturally become indecisive. This is precisely why it is so important to continuously monitor the market, to make this information available to all managers, and to discuss and clarify it regularly at all levels.

- **Inadequate resources**

There will not always be enough people or money to implement all the changes that may be needed. Middle managers must have the insight and the guts to sort out what is critical from what is merely desirable. In order to optimize available resources, these decisions need to be made collectively. An understanding of long-term market trends (and the organizational patterns and cultures needed to respond to these trends) can help in sorting out what most needs to be done.

- **Managers' styles, inclinations, and limitations**

This is mostly an educational and mentoring issue. Occasionally, however, some managers may need to be reassigned or let go because they are not able to deal with a new organizational culture. This needs to be fully understood and accepted by HR.

Staff Managers

Staff managers develop and operate the processes that support the core activity of an organization. These processes include finance, human resources, information systems, logistics, purchasing, marketing, communications, and so on. Collectively, these processes form an organization's infrastructure.

This infrastructure accounts for much more of an organization's activities than most leaders and managers realize. Indeed, these activities have a way of growing very large without attracting much attention. There needs to be a constant effort by top management to keep these activities from consuming too large a portion of total revenues.

Staff managers play a critical role in the business-matching process: they must constantly adjust what they do and how they work to fit the current business match. In order to do this, they must be kept constantly and clearly informed of what that match is. If they are not, they will automatically prepare for a wide range of contingencies—e.g., changes in sales, products, customer needs, etc. This is precisely what leads to unwarranted growth.

Consider the example of an information technology department, which looks vastly different in a Pioneer enterprise than it does in a Warrior organization. The former needs to provide technical information to inventors and entrepreneurs; the latter needs to focus on supporting and streamlining large-volume production. Understanding these different focuses and other differences among the four organizational types enables staff managers to offer the most effective support while remaining frugal.

The work of staff departments can be crucial to the proper positioning of an organization's products or services in the market. This is especially true in Jungle markets, where the infrastructure needed to meet customers' demands is essential to winning and keeping them. Logistics services, for example, ensure that customers get their orders on time. While this is important in all markets, superior proficiency is demanded in a Jungle, where customers have little or no brand loyalty and a one-day delay may be considered intolerable. (Think of the office supply business where many customers now expect same-day delivery.) Compare this to the Frontier, where lateness is sometimes excused because of the newness of a product or process and/or because of the lack of many alternatives.

Each staff manager needs to continuously examine their department's role within their organization and be aware of its position on the archetype grid so they can determine what needs to be adapted and improved.

To support the business-matching process, staff managers need to do the following:

1. Participate actively with middle managers in assessing their organization's position on the archetype grid as well as in developing appropriate operational strategies.
2. Determine the roles their departments need to play in supporting both the organization's strategic plan and its operational strategy.
3. Reach agreement with top management and other relevant managers on what is needed to create synchronicity between the organization's core processes and its infrastructure.
4. Continuously monitor the effectiveness of the support structures in relation to the organization's position on the archetype grid; develop and adapt support processes as necessary.
5. Help people in their support functions understand the moves, adaptations, and process improvements that will be necessary for success. Staff managers need to be clear about what benchmarks and measurements will be used and what attitudes and approaches will be most helpful.

As they perform these tasks, staff managers need to avoid or address these pitfalls:

- ***Entrenchment***

Support departments tend to develop cultures of their own. Not surprisingly, these are usually based on the styles and inclinations of the people who work in them. Over time, these mini cultures can become entrenched and closed to influences from the outside. The people in these cultures then routinely engage in the kind of political activity that is rewarded internally but is detrimental (or at best, valueless) to the larger organization. In addition, they may work, both individually and collectively, to ensure the department's survival by sharing only the information they want others to know. At times, they may even keep some of the most vital information to themselves.

These conditions steadily reinforce themselves and resist all efforts toward change. Those who attempt introspection and renewal are often eventually ostracized. Typically, managers are brought in from business line positions to change things, but people in the department may create an implicit plan to survive while that person is there without actually changing.

- *Low stature of staff managers*

In many organizations, the premier management roles are in business lines and/or core processes, and most top managers are chosen from this group (and perhaps from finance). Staff managers may therefore have little political stature and may not be included in serious strategizing. They may be brought in only after a strategy has already been decided upon, at which point they are simply told to comply and mobilize their resources.

This leaves staff managers in a position of supporting the organization but not sharing in any of the control. They are not part of the business-matching process no matter how supposedly open and explicit the organization's strategic planning may be.

- *Support departments that are too far ahead of the rest of the organization*

Some IT departments, for example, are so far ahead of the rest of their organizations technologically that they speak a different language and thus become politically isolated from other departments. These departments keep IT out of their meetings and strategy sessions and include its people only after the fact to create the electronic infrastructure needed to follow a strategy that has already been decided upon. This is, of course, far too late in the process and does not lead to creating the kind of support actually needed from IT. It also can result in bypassing those strategies that may well be the most beneficial, practical, or cost-effective.

Something similar can occur with human resources departments. HR managers sometimes feel that they possess a certain cultural enlightenment that core process people lack and that it is their mission to train these people to fit their vision. The core process people, of course, resist these efforts, which leads to HR's isolation from the real decision-making processes.

- ***Inappropriate integration of support structures and business lines***

Finding the correct way to integrate support activities with business lines is a critical design task but one which is not often performed well. The business-matching process can help a great deal here by providing direction to top and middle managers on the degree and type of integration needed to be successful in each market environment.

A Ruler needs to tie together its strongest independent parts in a way that maximizes the power of the business. This might be done through brand management, cross-division programs, shared innovation, and so on. It isn't especially easy to get these little fiefdoms to cooperate, let alone integrate; furthermore, it is important not to destroy the sense of ownership and power felt in each separate unit or department. Nevertheless, efficiencies are important to protect the large margins in a Kingdom market, and these can best be maintained through cross-functional and cross-divisional systems.

A Warrior should link together the many efforts of the organization to increase sales volume and the efficiency of production. It is important to constantly work to streamline production and, when possible, other systems as well. For example, special sales initiatives are often needed to stay a step ahead of the competition. However, these can become dangerously expensive if they are not integrated quickly and cooperatively in the field.

Hunters need to integrate systems that create a clear understanding of customer needs everywhere in the organization so that everyone in it can work to satisfy those needs. The relentless drive to lower costs will naturally create some integration and promote efficiency; however, it is crucial that the organization remain focused on being responsive to customer needs.

A Pioneer needs to tie together the loose parts of the system in a way that supports the innovation needed to get new products or services to market, all without seriously damaging the bottom line. The focus should be on obtaining needed resources and building appropriate technologies. Integration is not as crucial for a Pioneer as it is for the three other types of organizations because margins are usually sufficient to make up for inefficiencies (and in some cases, poor customer service). Furthermore, it is important not to tighten up the organization too much and thereby risk undermining the spirit of innovation. On the other hand, integration does typically lead to better service, greater efficiency, and more widespread acceptance in the market.

- *Mergers or acquisitions undertaken without significant involvement from staff managers*

All the research suggests that mergers and acquisitions rarely achieve anything close to their original purposes. Even though due diligence groups are used to identify and address potential legal issues and to make recommendations concerning the assimilation of one culture into another, most mergers and acquisitions run into serious problems involving the differences between the two cultures.

Often, this is because staff managers have been left out of the picture, but even when staff managers are included in a due diligence group, they are well aware that the merger or acquisition is driven by highly political considerations and involves many ego issues, particularly on the part of the acquirer. They know whether management really wants to purchase a company or not and will, more often than not, provide the information they know management wants to hear, despite whatever reservations they might have.

MBA Students and Programs

Organizations throughout the world have come to rely on MBA programs to prepare people to perform important leadership roles. In fact, in many organizations today, an MBA degree is a requirement for anyone wishing to be considered for upper management.

MBA programs would do well to teach the business-matching process as part of their leadership development programs for three reasons. First, all organizational leaders need to understand (and be able to identify) the four basic market environments and the four basic organizational types and cultures. Upper-level managers in particular need this skill for they will be directing the development of strategy, leading the implementation of plans and operational changes, and spearheading the redesign of their organizations' operations and cultures.

Second, every future leader must learn to navigate the rough seas of organizational politics. The business-matching process is a useful way to understand the basic political rules that govern each of the organizational archetypes.

Third, an MBA student considering a career in a particular organization can use the business-matching process as a tool to examine what that organization does and what kind of leadership role they might eventually be able to play in it. They can, of course, also do the same for entire industries, fields, and professions.

As they use the business-matching process, an MBA student needs to do the following:

1. Become familiar with the basic business-matching concepts and use them with real or imaginary organizations. These concepts will provide a new framework for understanding the issues of managing change and will become useful additions to their repertoire of strategic planning and organizational development skills.

2. Develop a clear sense of their own strengths, leadership style, and talents for working in each organizational archetype and for leading people from one archetype to another. This self-knowledge will help them focus their energies on those organizations and fields for which they are best suited. This, in turn, will help them avoid any dead ends and give them a leg up in ascending any organizational ladder.

3. Use the business-matching process to examine organizations where they currently work or are considering working, especially if they want to become leaders.

As they use the business-matching process, MBA students need to avoid or address these pitfalls:

• *MBA programs' limited focus on organizational issues*

Typically, what little is taught about organizational concerns focuses mainly on managing change. Even then, this usually means simply getting the organization to comply with the predetermined judgments and strategies of top management and/or minimizing the effects of downsizing.

• *Students' tendency to pick potential employers based on P/E ratios, stock prices, and other measurements that seem to promise stock options and large payoffs for top management*

MBA programs provide students with many tools for measuring value and profitability. None of these, however, tell students a thing about what it will actually be like to work for a particular organization.

• *The prevailing (but incorrect) view that a good manager can be a leader in almost any situation*

Certainly, there are some generic leadership skills that can be learned and applied to a wide variety of situations, but it is wishful thinking to believe in an all-encompassing leadership genius that works at all times in all organizations and situations.

Coaches and Consultants

The business-matching process can provide consultants, coaches, and managers with a shared language, a collective vision, and a common format for discovery. When I introduce the business-matching process in my own consulting work, I have found that a clear mutual understanding quickly develops. In addition, the models and language of the business-matching process naturally stimulate the exploration of options for organizational designs, cultures, and operations. Furthermore, the concepts of business-matching provide an easily accessible model for making decisions and planning strategy. The business-matching process also creates a framework for providing feedback to managers on their leadership skills.

Market information is vital to any organization, yet the *kind* of market information needed to make wise decisions is different for each organizational archetype. Thus, marketing consultants need to be conversant with the organizational implications of each market archetype. Similarly, organizational consultants need to be conversant with the market implications of each organizational type.

In using the business-matching process, coaches and consultants need to do the following:

1. *Introduce the business-matching process early on in any professional relationship.* This can then become the ground on which everything else is built or, alternatively, a backdrop against which other tools and concepts can be productively employed.
2. *Develop a clear understanding of where an organization, its markets, and its products and/or services fall on the archetype grid.* This needs to be done as early in the relationship as possible.
3. *Understand that the business-matching process adds to—and is not meant to replace—other tools and ideas.*

As they use the business-matching process, MBA students need to avoid or address these pitfalls:

- **Ignoring the organizational implications of strategic decisions**

Despite rhetoric to the contrary, many consulting firms have no real perspective from an organizational point of view. Their focus is typically on either strategy or operations; they are most concerned with plans, processes, activities, finances, markets, products, numbers of people, etc. Obviously, these are very important parts of any enterprise, but organizational structure and culture are at least as important as all the other concerns put together. Truly effective interventions involve both the technical and the human sides of an organization and address them together as a symbiosis.

- *The difficulties of measurement*

Intervening in an organization's culture and structure is a lot less measurable and concrete than intervening in operations. In addition, it demands a view of the whole system and an understanding of the interdependence of all its parts. This is often not appreciated by clients, yet the lack of such a view is one of the main reasons why large-scale interventions often fail (or create many new problems).

- *Fear of the organizational implications of one-to-one assistance*

Many coaches and consultants work at the subgroup level. They coach managers, assist in team building, train departments in needed skills, or help with specific programs such as process redesign. Some become temporary parts of the existing system. These people are usually oblivious to the implications of their work in terms of the larger organizational system. Indeed, most do not wish to know or be influential beyond the specific tasks they are hired to perform.

Yet when coaching a manager or redesigning a process, the consultant needs to understand the current business match (or mismatch) so they can best assist their client in performing the idiosyncratic tasks most appropriate for that particular type of market and organization.

For example, imagine that you are counseling a manager in a Warrior company who is under great stress because she is not comfortable in such a rigid environment. If you knew nothing about organizational archetypes, you might counsel her to speak with her boss and try to create a plan for making her situation less rigid. This plan would of course fail, however, because what would be good for her would be bad for the organization. Eventually, she would probably leave the company on her own but with much resentment toward her boss and perhaps with a reputation for being a complainer and a weakling.

In contrast, your knowledge of the organizational archetypes would enable you to quickly see that this manager is simply in the wrong type of organization. The rigidity that so bothers her is appropriate for her Warrior enterprise and should not be changed to suit her. Rather, she should seek out a Ruler or Pioneer organization that will offer her more latitude in her action and decisions. And when she does leave her current job, it will be without resentment, regret, or dishonor.

- *Managers and organizations that view strategic planning as short-term business planning dressed up with highbrow words*

Many OD interventions rely heavily on client information and processes to arrive at strategic goals and plans for improvement. Clients use many excellent tools to create this information; however, without the business-matching process as a complement, the context for deciding on a strategic direction may be inadequate. To create a truly strategic plan, it is imperative that the market be understood in relation to the kind of organization that can best succeed in it.

- *Seeing business-matching as a one-time event rather than as a process*

Evaluating an organization against its markets doesn't happen just once. Markets, customer needs, and competition are all changing constantly; macro changes also occur as organizations, products, and services mature and journey from one archetype to another. *Thus consultants and coaches must emphasize that the business-matching process needs to occur regularly if not continuously.*

Do not assume that an organization will *get it right* once and for all by going through the process a single time. The business-matching process is a long-term commitment and an integral element in an organization's long-term success.

Beginning the Journey

When your organization and its market are in proper alignment, there is a palpable feeling of *rightness* that flows through the entire system. It is much like the hum of a sailboat when the lines are set just right and the sails are in perfect trim. Any experienced sailor can tell you about this sound and the sense of flow that goes with it.

Your training in the business-matching process is now complete. You have everything you need to begin creating this same sense of flow and alignment in your own organization.

It's time to push off, grab the rudder, and set sail.

Bon voyage.

Note to the Academic Reader:

Readers of Sync & Swim who are interested in the substantive research that this assessment process represents will find the next few pages useful in pursuing the origins of this discussion on the dynamics of competition and organization. The review was done as part of a study which is documented at the end of the list and reviewed by the AMA.

The bibliography is also provided to assist in examining the appropriateness of the process.

THE ARCHETYPE
ASSESSMENT INVENTORY

Relevant Literature

Literature Review

In the 1950s, researchers introduced contingency theory into the study of management and organizational behavior. Contingency theory recognizes that organizations are open systems that survive according to a cycle of receiving inputs from the environment, internal transformation of inputs into outputs, and reception of feedback from the environment so that adjustments in the system are made (Morgan 1997). Applied to the study of organizations, the assumption upon which contingency theory is based is that "organizational variables are in a complex interrelationship with one another and with conditions in the environment" (Lawrence and Lorsch 1986, 157); therefore, when an organization's structure and processes are in harmony with environmental conditions, the organization is more likely to be successful (Lawrence and Lorsch 1986). Contingency theory shifted the focus of organizational and management research from identifying ideal organizational structures, management techniques, technologies, and strategies to explaining how such organizational characteristics should be adjusted to maximize the fit between an organization and its environment (e.g., Burns and Stalker 1961; Child 1972; Duncan 1972; Lawrence and Lorsch 1986; Miles and Snow 1978; Thompson 1967; Woodward 1965) (Morgan 1997).

Environmental Analysis

An organization's external environment is defined as "the totality of physical and social factors [outside the organization] that are taken into consideration in the decision-making behavior of individuals in the organization" (Duncan 1972, 314). Two divergent approaches have been utilized extensively to measure competitive environments. One stream of research has relied on objective industry data while the other has relied upon managers' perceptions of environmental dimensions. One reviewer acknowledged that recent studies are utilizing objective measures more often than perceptual measures (see Bluedorn 1993). Most studies using objective indicators aggregate data at the industry level—for example, profits, concentration ratios, or growth in sales—as measure of dynamism or munificence. A few studies use measures that are specific for a firm (Dess and Rasheed 1991). Objective measures may be important for understanding environmental constraints affecting the organization's strategic choices (Boyd, Dess, and Rasheed 1993).

Objective measures, however, may not provide a valid indication of the environments in which managers maneuver and negotiate. An objective measure does not capture the perceptions, knowledge, and beliefs held by managers concerning the environment (Walsh, Henderson, and Deighton 1988). Weick (1969) argued that "objective" environments do not exist; rather, environments are enacted through perceptions. Weick (1969) reasoned that achieving an appropriate fit requires that the organization's leaders must accurately perceive environmental conditions in order to select the most appropriate strategies (Boyd et al. 1993). One researcher asserts that "one's manager's threat is another's opportunity" (Starbuck 1976). Bluedorn (1993) states that environmental uncertainty is a *misnomer* "because the uncertainty was not in the environment [but] in the perceptions of managers in terms of their ability to predict the future environmental states" (p. 166). Others suggest that managers respond only to their perceptions since conditions that are not perceived do not affect managers' decisions (Anderson and Paine 1975; Pfeffer and Salancik 1978; Weick 1969).

Dimensions of the Environment

Most researchers view the environment as a multidimensional construct (Bluedorn 1993; Duncan 1972). The dimensions most consistently utilized are complexity, dynamism, uncertainty, and munificence (Bluedorn 1993). Duncan's (1972) study identified environmental characteristics that contribute to perceptions of environmental uncertainty. Uncertainty was calculated on the basis of two environmental dimensions: (a) the number of external factors taken into consideration in the decision-making process (simple [few factors considered] versus complex [many factors considered]) and (b) the degree to which these factors were changing or remained the same (static [little or no change] versus dynamic [continuous change]). He found that the amount of change in the environmental factors contributed more to perceptions of uncertainty than the complexity of the organization's environment.

Complexity. The simple-complex dimension (complexity) refers to the number of environmental components considered when making a decision. One way to operationalize complexity is by counting the number of environmental components that respondents have labeled as "important" in their decision-making efforts (Duncan 1972; Pfeiffer and Salancik 1978). Importance is most often related to the resource-based perspective (Daft Sormunen and Parks 1988). The most important components are often perceived to provide the most critical resources or opportunities that may lead to a strategic advantage or produce the most severe threats to the organization's profitability or survival (Boyd and Fulk 1996).

The effects of environmental complexity are not entirely understood. Some experts have suggested that complexity forces managers to utilize greater rationality to link and understand complex environments while others contend that "complexity may lead to greater use of cognitive simplification processes such as selective perception, heuristics, and analogies, which in turn may . . . potentially restrict the range of alternatives considered and the information used to evaluate them" (Goll and Rasheed 1997, 584).

Dynamism. The static-dynamic dimension (dynamism) refers to the rate of change in the environmental components perceived by the decision maker. Duncan measured dynamism by asking respondents how frequently each component of the environment changed. His response categories ranged from never to very often. Management theorists have presumed that as the rate of change increases, predictability of conditions and outcomes decreases, thereby creating uncertainty (Boyd and Fulk 1996; Goll and Rasheed 1997).

Uncertainty. Uncertainty, absence of information about events in the environment, is another dimension that researchers incorporate into environmental studies (Boyd and Fulk 1996; Daft et al. 1988). Duncan (1972) suggested that uncertainty results from and varies according to the complexity of the environment and the rate of change in the components of the environment. Studies investigating perceived environmental uncertainty have followed Duncan (1972) in assuming that uncertainty is caused by complexity and change; therefore, uncertainty has often been calculated indirectly by multiplying complexity scores by the perceived rate of change. Daft et al. (1988) believed that the relative importance of components is a critical dimension of environmental analysis and factored importance into the composite scores of uncertainty. Other researchers have assumed that uncertainty is equivalent to the rate of change in the environment (Goll and Rasheed 1997; Rajagopalan, Rasheed, and Datta 1993).

Munificence. The fourth dimension, munificence, is the extent to which the environment can support sustained growth (Dess and Beard 1984) and provide organizational slack (Bourgeois 1981). Organizational slack is a "cushion of actual or potential resources which allows an organization to adapt successfully to . . . external pressures . . . [and] to initiate changes in strategy with respect to the external environment" (Bourgeois 1981, 30). When slack is low, strategic choices are limited (Porter 1980). Munificence has been operationalized as the number of competitors in the environment (Dess and Beard 1984).

Studies investigating the effects of perceived complexity, dynamism, uncertainty, and munificence have produced inconsistent results (Gerloff, Muir, and Bodensteiner 1991; Milliken 1987). According to Goll and Rasheed (1997), complexity and munificence, which are critical dimensions of an organization's environment, have been largely ignored in recent studies. They point out that munificence in an uncertain environment is quite different from munificence in a more stable environment. Despite the large number of studies investigating the relationship between strategy, structure, and external environments (for a complete review, see Bluedorn 1993 and Bluedorn, Johnson, Cartwright, and Barringer 1994), researchers have failed to develop an instrument that adequately operationalizes organizational environments for business enterprises (Boyd et al. 1993; Buchko 1994; Dess and Rasheed 1991). Therefore, some authors have demanded that attention should be devoted to developing valid and reliable scales to measure organizational environments (Boyd et al. 1993; Dess and Rasheed 1991) "in order to build a comprehensive, coherent literature about the environment and its impact on the [organization]" (Sharfman and Dean 1991, 681). The instrument upon which this study is based measures managers' perceptions of the competitive environment on all four of the dimensions: complexity, dynamism, uncertainty, and munificence. The instrument includes twenty questions, five questions for each dimension.

Linking Environments with Organizational Characteristics

Many studies since the 1960s have suggested that links exist between organizational environments and appropriate organizational characteristics. Morgan (1997) stated, "We notice that certain species of organization are better 'adapted' to specific environmental conditions than others" (p. 33). In investigating organizational characteristics appropriate for various environmental conditions, researchers have considered the degree of centralization in decision making (Burns and Stalker 1961; Chandler 1962; Fouraker cited in Lawrence and Lorsch 1986), formality of the organizational structure, as well as type of organizational structure such as mechanistic versus organic (Burns and Stalker 1961; Hall 1962; Lawrence and Lorsch 1986), degree of functional specialty, and communication patterns across functions (Chandler 1962; Galbraith 1973; Woodward 1965), the extent to which members' behaviors are controlled by rules and procedures (Burns and Stalker 1961; Lawrence and Lorsch 1987), the openness of the planning process (Lindsay and Rue 1980), the length of the planning horizon (Das 1987; Lindsay and Rue 1980; Terreberry 1968), and the types of strategies that best fit environmental conditions (Chandler 1962;

Fouraker cited in Lawrence and Lorsch 1986; Galbraith 1973; Paine and Anderson 1977).

Chandler (1962) was among the first to suggest that companies should adjust their strategy to match the environment, either to protect current market share or to take advantage of product and market opportunities. Using case studies, he demonstrated that successful strategy execution requires an organizational structure that supports the implementation of the chosen strategy.

Numerous studies have shown that organizational characteristics best suited for stable environments include a more formalized mechanistic organizational structure, where tasks and authority of each function are clearly defined. In mechanistic structures, decision making is centralized and member behaviors are controlled by enforcement of rules and procedures (Burns and Stalker 1961; Chandler 1962; Lawrence and Lorsch 1986; Miles and Snow 1978), and communication across functions is limited to appropriate hierarchical channels (Burns and Stalker 1961). According to Galbraith (1973), when organizations operate in stable environments, managers can develop procedures and rules to control members' behaviors by specifying appropriate responses. As unique situations arise, the situation is referred to a manager high enough in the organizational hierarchy to have adequate information to understand how various courses of action will affect various subunits within the organization; this manager has the task of identifying appropriate behaviors to handle the situation for the benefit of the overall organization.

Conversely, organizations in rapidly changing environments require less formal, more organic structures. According to Galbraith (1973), uncertainty limits the managers' ability to preplan; therefore, Terreberry (1968) concluded that in uncertain environments, planning horizons are shorter than in more certain environments. Galbraith (1973) explained how uncertainty in the environment increases the amount of information that must be processed within organizations, which subsequently determines which organizational structure the organization should choose. "The greater the task uncertainty, the greater the amount of information that must be processed among decision makers during task execution in order to achieve a given level of performance" (Galbraith 1973, 4). In organic organizations, due to instability in the environment, tasks cannot be clearly defined and assigned and rules and procedures are not as useful as in a stable environment; therefore, the organization is less formally organized and has more decentralized decision making. The assumption is that in order to accomplish the organization's tasks, individuals must be knowledgeable of the organization's goals and understand how their efforts are related others' activities throughout the organization. Galbraith (1973) and Chandler (1962) both recognized the limitations of hierarchical structures for handling increasing numbers of unique situations. They suggested that in unstable environments, employees at lower levels of the organization must be given more discretion to solve problems. Therefore, individuals in these environments should be free to communicate with each other regardless of one's vertical rank in the organization (Burns and Stalker 1961; Chandler 1962; Lawrence and Lorsch 1986).

According to Fouraker (cited in Lawrence and Lorsch 1986), environments that include rapidly changing elements create a munificent environment, which is favorable because rapidly changing elements—such as changes in technology, economic conditions, or demographic shifts—create new resources and/or new opportunities for organizations to exploit while an unfavorable environment is a stable environment where resources are static and therefore relatively scarce. Such an environment leads to fierce competition among organizations for limited resources. Fouraker's research identified two dichotomous types of organizations: *L* and *T* organizations. *L* organizations are viewed as traditional bureaucracies that rely on rigid rules and authoritarian managers. In an *L* organization, threats from the external environment provide a common uniting purpose for organizational members. Due to the focus on external threats, internal conflict is viewed as threatening to the organization's survival and is not tolerated. The best organizational structure in an unfavorable environment is an authoritarian hierarchy with a single leader and a clear chain of command (Fouraker cited in Lawrence and Lorsch 1986).

On the other hand, organizations in munificent environments (*T* organizations) require independent technical experts exchanging information to increase members' learning, which in turn leads to innovative ways to take advantage of opportunities in the environment. *T* organizations are characterized by limited hierarchy, where most work is accomplished and coordinated by committees. In these organizations, formal disciplinary procedures are not necessary because conflict often leads to discovery and professional specialists are more likely to use self-discipline or peer-imposed discipline. Success occurs when independent specialists identify environmental opportunities and develop the means for the organization to pursue opportunities (Fouraker cited in Lawrence and Lorsch 1986). Similarly, Chandler observed that "strategic growth resulted from an awareness of the opportunities and needs . . . created by changing population, income, and technology . . . to employ existing or expanding resources more profitably" (Chandler 1962, 15).

Duncan (1972) identified four types of environments: (a) simple-static, (b) simple-dynamic, (c) complex-static, and (d) complex-dynamic. When Duncan compared the types of organizations in each of his four environment types, he discovered that no research and development organizations were in the simple-static environment and that no manufacturing firms were in the complex-dynamic environment, which led him to conclude that different types of organizations operate in different types of environments. Similarly, Hall (1962) found that research and development departments utilized an organic organization while production departments were more mechanistic.

Lindsay and Rue (1980) found that as external environments become more complex and uncertain, large firms tend to use more openness in their long-range planning processes, but small firms tend to use less openness. "This possibly suggests that the top management of small firms tends to centralize planning under adverse conditions and to trust more in their own judgments, but managers in large firms tend to be more open to information from as many sources as possible" (Lindsay and Rue 1980, 402). They also found that the external environment becomes for complex and uncertain, firms had a longer history of utilizing long-range planning techniques, shorter review periods, and shorter goals.

Chandler (1962) observed that in the face of environmental changes, organizations could choose a defensive strategy or a positive strategy. Firms adopting defensive strategies are trying to protect their current market share while firms adopting positive strategies are actively seeking new product and market opportunities. Miles and Snow (1978) identified four strategic orientations: defenders, prospectors, analyzers, and reactors. Each orientation has a different perspective on three universal organizational problems, identifying product markets, selecting an appropriate technology, and structuring the organization to facilitate implementation of the chosen strategy. Defenders, as the name implies, are primarily interested in protecting existing markets by reducing costs through improved efficiency and rarely invest in research and development. Prospectors focus on exploiting new market opportunities; therefore, they stress research and development. Analyzers are viewed as combining the characteristics of both defenders and analyzers while reactors simply react to market conditions and rarely choose a competitive strategy.

REFERENCES

Anderson, C. R. and F. T. Paine. 1975. "Managerial Perceptions and Strategic Behavior." *Academy of Management Journal* 18: 811–823.

Bluedorn, A. C. 1993. "Pilgrim's Progress: Trends and Convergence in Research on Organizational Size and Environments." *Journal of Management* 19 (2): 163–191.

Bluedorn, A. C., R. A. Johnson, D. K. Cartwright, and B. R. Barringer. 1994. "The Interface and Convergence of the Strategic Management and Organizational Environment Domains." *Journal of Management* 20 (2): 201–262.

Bongiorno, L. 1993. "Raise Your Hand if You're Sure Business Strategy Is Being Taught in American Business School." *Journal of Business Strategy* 14 (5): 36–41.

Bourgeois, L. J. 1981. "On the Measurement of Organizational Slack." *Academy of Management Review* 6: 29–39.

Boyd, B. K., G. G. Dess, and A. M. A. Rasheed. 1993. "Divergence between Archival and Perceptual Measures of the Environment: Causes and Consequences." *Academy of Management Review* 18 (2): 204–226.

Boyd, B. K. and J. Fulk. 1996. "Executive Scanning and Perceived Uncertainty: A Multidimensional Model." *Journal of Management* 22 (1): 1–21.

Buchko, A. A. 1994. "Conceptualization and Measurement of Environmental Uncertainty: An Assessment of the Miles and Snow Perceived Environmental Uncertainty Scale." *Academy of Management Journal* 37: 410–425.

Burns, T. and G. M. Stalker. 1961. *The Management of Innovation.* London: Tavistock Publications.

Chandler, Arthur. 1962. *Strategy and Structure: Chapters in the History of Industrial Enterprise.* Cambridge: MIT Press.

Child, J. 1972. "Organization Structure, Environment and Performance: The Role of Strategic Choice." *Sociology* 6 (1): 1–22.

Daft, R. L., J. Sormunen, and D. Parks. 1988. "Chief Executive Scanning, Environmental Characteristics, and Company Performance: An

Empirical Study." *Strategic Management Journal* 9: 123–139. *Strategic Management Journal* 8: 259–277.

Das, T. K. 1987. "Strategic Planning and Individual Temporal Orientation." *Strategic Management Journal* 8: 203–209.

Dess, G. G. and D. W. Beard. 1984. "Dimensions of Organizational Task Environments." *Administrative Science Quarterly* 29: 52–73.

Dess, G. G. and A. M. A. Rasheed. 1991. "Conceptualizing and Measuring Organizational Environments: A Critique and Suggestions." *Journal of Management* 17 (4): 701–710.

Duncan, R. B. 1972. "Characteristics of Organizational Environments and Perceived Environmental Uncertainty." *Administrative Science Quarterly*: 313–327.

Galbraith, J. 1973. *Designing Complex Organizations*. Reading, Massachusetts: Addison-Wesley Publishing Company.

Gerloff, E. A., N. K. Muir, and W. D. Bodensteiner. 1991. "Three Components of Perceived Environmental Uncertainty: An Exploratory Analysis of the Effects of Aggregation." *Journal of Management* 17: 749–768.

Goll, I. and A. M. A. Rasheed. 1997. "Rational Decision-Making and Firm Performance: The Moderating Role of Environment." *Strategic Management Journal* 18 (7): 583–591.

Hall, R. H. 1962. "Intraorganizational Structure Variation." *Administrative Science Quarterly*: 295–308.

Lawrence, P. R. and J. W. Lorsch. 1986. *Organizations and Environments: Managing Differentiation and Integration*. Boston, Massachusetts: Harvard Business School Press.

Lindsay, W. M. and L. W. Rue. 1980. "Impact of Organization Environment on the Long-Range Planning Process: A Contingency View." *Academy of Management Journal* 23: 385–404.

Miles, R. E. and C. C. Snow. 1978. *Organizational Strategy, Structure and Process*. Boston, Massachusetts: McGraw-Hill.

Miller, D. and P. H. Friesen. 1977. "Strategy Making in Context: Ten Empirical Archetypes." *The Journal of Management Studies*: 253–280.

Milliken, F. J. 1987. "Three Types of Perceived Uncertainty About the Environments: State, Effect, and Response Uncertainty." *Academy of Management Review* 12: 133–143.

Mintzberg, H. 1975. "The Manager's Job: Folklore and Fact." *Harvard Business Review*: 49–61.

Morgan, Gareth. 1997. *Images of Organizations*. Thousand Oaks, California: Sage Publications, Inc.

Pfeffer, J. and G. R. Salancik. 1978. *The External Control of Organizations: A Resource Dependence Perspective*. New York: Harper & Row.

Porter, M. E. 1980. *Competitive Strategy: Techniques for Analyzing Industries and Competitors*. New York: Free Press.

Rajagopalan, N. A., M. A. Rasheed, and D. K. Datta. 1993. "Strategic Decision Processes: Critical Review and Future Directions." *Journal of Management* 19 (3): 349–384.

Sharfman, M. P. and J. W. Dean, Jr. 1991. "Conceptualizing and Measuring the Organizational Environment: A Multidimensional Approach." *Journal of Management* 17 (4): 681–700.

Shrock, S. A. and W. C. C. Coscarelli. 1989. *Criterion-Referenced Test Development*. Reading, Massachusetts: Addison-Wesley Publishing Company Inc.

Starbuck, W. H. 1976. "Organizations and Their Environments." In *Handbook of Industrial Psychology*, edited by M. D. Dunnette. Chicago: Rand McNally.

Terreberry, S. 1968. "The Evolution of Organizational Environments." *Administrative Science Quarterly* 12: 590–613.

Tompson, G. H. and P. Dass. 2000. "Improving Students' Self-Efficacy in Strategic Management: The Relative Impact of Cases and Simulations." *Simulation and Gaming* 31 (1): 22–41.

Thompson, J. D. 1967. *Organizations in Action*. New York: McGraw-Hill Book Co.

Thompson, A. A. and A. J. Strickland. 2003. *Strategic Management: Concepts and Cases*. Boston, Massachusetts: McGraw-Hill Irwin.

Walsh, J., C. Henderson, and J. Deighton. 1988. "Negotiated Belief Structures and Decision Performance: An Empirical Investigation." *Organizational Behavior and Human Decision Processes* 42: 194–216.

Weick, K. E. 1969. *The Social Psychology of Organizing*. Reading, Massachusetts: Addison-Wesley.

Woodward, Joan. 1965. *Industrial Organization: Theory and Practice*. London: Oxford University Press.

By Marjorie L. Icenogle, Department of Management, University of South Alabama, Mobile, Alabama; Bruce W. Eagle, Department of Management and Marketing, St. Cloud State University, St. Cloud, Minnesota; and Norman B. Bryan, Department of Management, Georgia State University, Atlanta, Georgia.

Academics that have contributed and/or recommend this book:

- Norman B. Bryan, PhD, Department of Management, Georgia State University
- David Christopherson, PhD, School of Business, Hamline University
- Bruce W. Eagle, PhD, Department of Management and Marketing, St. Cloud State
- Manuel Teles Fernandes, MBA, principal, Gestao Totale, Lisbon, Portugal
- Dennis Gallagher, PhD, Organization Development Network
- Frank Hoy, director, Collaborative for Entrepreneurship and Innovation, School of Business; Paul R. Beswick Professor of Innovation and Entrepreneurship, Worcester Polytecnic Institute
- Tom Hubler, president, Hubler for Business Families, St. Paul, Minnesota
- Margorie L. Icenogle, PhD, Department of Management, University of South Alabama
- Carter McNamara, PhD, Authenticity Consulting, Carlson School, University of Minnesota
- Soumodip Sakar, PhD, Universidade de Evora, Evora, Portugal
- Andrew Van De Ven, PhD, Vernon H. Heath Chair of Organization Innovation and Management, Carlson School, University of Minnesota

Previous Publications by Jack Tesmer

Your Perfect Business Match, published by Career Press in 2001 (published in China in 2003 by Science and Culture Press)
De Overlevers, published by De Management Biblioteek, Amsterdam, Brussels, 1995

Other Books and Pamphlets by Jack through the Jack Tesmer Institute

Sailing Guide for Managers: Markets
Sailing Guide for Managers: Organization
Sailing Guide for Managers: Snapshots
Shipbuilding for Managers: Organization
Market Centric Organization Dimension Assessment: An Examination of Energy, Synergy, and Core Value Organizational Dynamics
Creating Strategy That Works: 9-Block Strategy Model
The Dynamics of Exit as a Process

Edwards Brothers Malloy
Thorofare, NJ USA
February 9, 2015